Marriage, A Miracle of Completion

Marriage, a Miracle of Completion

*Learn, Practice & Pray Your Ways
to a Successful Marital Lifestyle*

Harry Mogaji

Best wishes

by the Author:
Charles Soyoye
Soyoye 11/6/20.

Charles O. Soyoye

To order additional copies of this book, contact:
Xlibris Corporation
0-800-644-6988
www.xlibrispublishing.co.uk
Orders@xlibrispublishing.co.uk
303448

CONTENTS

Why Revise, Marriage a Miracle of Completion?......9

The End......11

Introduction......13

1. What You Must Know About Marriage 21
2. The Marriage Institution......31
3. The True Meaning of Love 36
4. Illustration of the Difference Between a Man and a Woman......43
5. Divorce is an Abuse......52
6. Believe the Word of God, and Not Your Situation!......57
7. You are What You Watch 70
8. Choice of a Spouse......73
9. Speak the Language of Blessing of Peace......82
10. All in the Family 88
11. Godly Offspring......91
12. Encouraging Your Children to Bring Out the Best in Them 102
13. Good Manners and True Education Begin At Home! 107
14. Secrets of Keeping Your Fight Fair and Your Marriage Strong 111
15. Avoid Destructive Temptation 118
16. Marriage and Money......127
17. Marriage is a Blessing and a Privilege From God 131
18. Factors that Will Help Your Marriage Succeed......137
19. Reasons Why Two People are Better Than One......144
20. Marriage Mentors 146

I BELIEVE

You can have a successful marital life
you want, if you will just help your
spouse enough get what
he or she wants.

WHY REVISE, MARRIAGE A MIRACLE OF COMPLETION?

To be candid, I wrestled with whether or not I should publish a revision of marriage a miracle of completion. However, I believe there are some compelling reasons for updating and making critical changes in the book. Firstly, I felt I could make information substantially more helpful and less controversial as far as the husband and wife relationship is concerned.

Secondly, I felt that it was important to update some things that have changed since marriage a miracle of completion was written. I have the strong feeling that I could make the book better by the grace of God, even with the world financial crisis affecting families, compelled me to make the changes, so that husband and wife can receive encouragement through the Word of God and stay together in Christ Jesus.

To bring you up to date from a family perspective, Oladunni (my wife) and I just celebrated our 22nd year wedding anniversary. We have 3 boys, (Damisola, Damola and Debola.) Oladunni and I spend more time together, pray more together than ever before because our sons are all big boys. I still find it difficult to believe that I have been blessed with such a beautiful family, starting with my wonderful wife God gave me back in 1990. We are more in love, do more things together, communicate more effectively and have more fun than ever.

To God is the Glory.
Amen.

THE END

I am sure that this is an unusual way to start a book, but this is an "unusual piece of work." This book is all about you, your family, and your future. It will encourage you how to be a blessing to yourself, your family, your future and how you can get more out of all of them by giving more to each of them directly or indirectly.

I believe that this is the end, or at least the beginning of the end of negative thinking, negative action, and negative reaction; the end of defeatism and despondency; the end of settling for less than you deserve to have and are capable of obtaining; the end of being influenced by narrow minded people with little minds thinking little thoughts about trivia that is the stock and trade of Mr. & Mrs. mediocrity.

May I say this, on your behalf; it is the end of the world most deadly family disease called "Divorce" and hardening of attitudes and behaviours. I want everyone reading this book to understand that marriage is the idea of God for a family. Hear what the bible says, "Except the Lord builds the house, they labour in vain who build it; except the Lord keeps the city, the watchman wakes but in vain." (Psalms 127:1.)

You are born to win in every area of your life, as well as your marriage. That is why marriage a miracle of completion book is written just for you, so that you can be fulfilled in your marital relationship in Jesus name.

Amen!

INTRODUCTION

The purpose of this book is to encourage both husband and wife that God is still the Originator of the institution of marriage. Marriage is the relationship between a man and a woman whose primary purpose is to raise offspring. Marriage unites a man and a woman as husband and wife. It encompasses and built upon spiritual, physical, sexual, economical and emotional bonds. Married couples are bound to protect one another and in so doing avoid choices and actions which are harmful to them and members of their family.

I believe marriage provides a secure and stable place to pursue innate desire for inner peace, tranquility and happiness. The marriage covenant requires both husband and wife to protect, care and nurture the children who are part of the family. To many people, marriage entails different meaning. True marriage that God ordained is based on loving relationship between a man and a woman in which both of them made a vow to live together "for better for worse, for richer for poorer, in sickness and in health till death do them part".

One of the secret of a successful marital life is for God to give you the right person and being the right person to your spouse. Finding your ideal partner is a never-to-be—forgotten memory that you find your Mr. or Mrs. right you have been praying to find. But this is just the first step to a long and successful relationship. I believe being the right person in love and adapting to your marriage situation is more significant in a successful relationship than everything else in marriage. However, many people did not realize the true essence of this wisdom of perfect match and patience until everything is deteriorated due to lack of understanding and mental compatibility.

May I say that it is important nowadays for you to know your partner well enough and try as much as possible to change for the best; step by step in the pace of your marital life. You have to understand that the truth of marriage success is not only finding the right partner alone, but being the right person too with genuine love, commitment, endurance, patience, understanding concern and loyalty. I pray that all these ingredients put together will help you achieve a successful marital life in Jesus name. Amen

The Bible says, "So God created man in his own image, in the image of God He created him, male and female He created them."(Genesis 1:27.) God saw that His work was not complete in that man was not complete and could not reproduce his kind alone; so, He made a help meet for him to enable him to propagate his kind. Hear what the Bible says, "And the Lord God said, "It is not good for the man to be alone. I will make a companion who will help him."(Genesis 2:18.)

A help suitable to man intellectually, morally, and physically as his counterpart! The Word of God did not say a helper that will dominate him; a helper that will always nag him, fight him always, or a helper that will always criticize his decision making. Wait a minute! Are you saying that God created you in the wrong gender as a woman instead of a man?

Truth be told; you either believe the Word of God or you don't believe it at all. There is no in-between in the Word of God or you just believe the one that suits you best in the Bible. It does not work that way. You have to believe everything in the Bible because it is the Word of truth. Hear what the Bible says, "God blessed them and told them," Multiply and fill the earth and subdue it. Be masters over the fish and the birds and all animals."(Genesis 1:28.)

May I submit the truth of the Word of God to you today? "Nevertheless, in (the plan of) the Lord and from His point of view woman is not apart from and independent of man, nor is man aloof from and independent of woman. For as woman was made from man, even so man is also born of woman and all (whether male or female go forth) from God, (as their Author)." (1 Corinthians 11:11-12.) Everyone has to understand that the woman needed to co-operate fully with her husband and keep the customs as being equally blessed of God.

Both husband and wife have to recognize that the marriage institution is under attack in these modern times especially in western countries. There are negative forces out there that destroy marriages mostly in Christian's homes. These evil force causes many homes to break up, especially families that do not watch and pray together. The devil uses modernization lies, insignificant issues to blindfold and he magnifies lies to ensure husband and wife do not stand on the Word of God to agree together on any issue facing them. The Bible says, "Then Adam said. This (creature) is now bone of my bones and flesh of my flesh; she shall be called Woman, because she was taken out of a man. Therefore a man shall leave his father and mother and shall become united and cleave to his wife, and they shall become one flesh." (Genesis 2: 23-24.)

May I encourage everyone reading this book to understand that it literally means a woman is a she-man; womb-man; man with the womb; or female-man, because she was taken out of man. Woman is said not to have been taken out of man's head to be lorded over by him, nor from his feet to be trampled on him, but from his side to be equal with him, from under his arm to be protected by him, and from near his heart to be loved by him, (Genesis 3:16.) I believe that the fall of man does not cancel the original plan of God to replenish the earth with natural people. It only postpones it until the time of the Restitution of all things according to the Word of God.

Then all things will continue as they would have been if man had not fallen. If one can imagine how wonderful the world would have been if sin and the curse had not come upon it and then transfer that image to the New Earth, one would fully understand the eternal condition of the earth. Children would be born eternally and natural life would continue perpetually. All phases of natural life as before the fall will be fully realized forever. (Act 3:21.)

Hear what the Bible says, "But we are looking forward to the new heavens and new earth he has promised, a world where everyone is right with God." (2 Peter 3:13.) With all these in mind, it is paramount that we know and understand the truth of the Word of God. Jesus said to the Jews that believe on Him, "And you will know the truth, and the truth will set you free" (John 8:32.) Jesus exhorts believers to continue in His Word as this is the secret of freedom from sin, sickness, and all the curses of this life that Christ died to set us free from.

I want every man to understand the reason given why God does not accept their offerings. This is due to men dealing treacherously with the wives of their youth, their companions by covenant. God made two persons out of one in the beginning, i.e. the man and his wife; and had He wanted more than one wife for man He would have created more at that time.

For the Bible says, "Didn't the Lord make you one with your wife? In body and spirit you are his. And what does he want? Godly children from your union! So guard yourself; remain loyal to the wife of your youth. "For I hate divorce!" says the Lord, the God of Israel. It is as cruel as putting on a victim's bloodstained coat, says the Lord Almighty. "So guard yourself; always remain loyal to your wife." For the Lord, the God of Israel says: "I hate divorce and marital separation and him who cover his garment (his wife) with violence." Therefore keep a watch upon your spirit that it may be controlled by the Holy Spirit and deal not treacherously and faithlessly with your marriage mate." (Malachi 2:15-16.) God expresses His hatred of divorce very strongly and clearly.

The devil knows that God hates divorce, and that is why he is using all sorts of tricks and lies to destroy marriages. The devil lies to the modern world and calls all bad things good: creating gay or lesbian clergy, using media hype about sex education in schools, and presenting same-sex marriages as cool. The devil is a liar. The devil is lying to young people that living together (cohabiting) or having sex before marriage is cool. The government is encouraging single parenthood, especially single mother by telling women that a father is not important in raising a child.

The devil is using the people in government, and the media to lie to women that they need greater economic independence. In reality, many women do not just want a provider, they want a lover, a confidant, equal and a friend but many have forgotten that marriage is not a consumer choice such that if it does not work, you replace it. People have forgotten that marriage is the idea of God and there is a reason for creating marriage and there are blessings that go with it.

Marriage is eternal and a divine institution ordained by God and that is the reason Jesus answered the Pharisees trying to trap Him with their question on divorce for every cause. "Haven't you read the scriptures?" Jesus replied. "They record that from the beginning, God made them male and female." (Matthew 19:4). Furthermore Jesus gave them a warning that, "Since they are no longer two but one, let no one separate them, for God has joined them together."(Matthew 19:6.) The fact is that God recognizes all legal marriages and will hold each man and woman responsible for their vows.

Marriage is by example of Adam and Eve from the beginning of creation. You need to understanding that marriage makes a man and a woman one flesh, with complete union of interest, fortunes, desires, joys, and sorrows in a lasting partnership. People should realize the evil consequence of divorce for themselves, their children and others who become entangled in sin by it. Everyone must understand that any man who divorces his wife and marries another woman commits adultery unless his wife has been marital unfaithful; and vice versa.

Marriage generally is a contract between two people, i.e. (a man and a woman) but in Biblical sense, marriage is a covenant relationship between two people (man and woman) and their God. In a contract, two people involved can legitimately dissolve the contract if it's not in their best interests to continue and each goes their way. However in Christian doctrine, marriage is not a contract but a covenant; a covenant cannot be legitimately broken.

Anyone with the fear of God in him or her does not act that way; for what did that one do, who was seeking offspring from God? So watch out for your feelings lest you be unfaithful to the wife of your youth. I believe that marriage can be broken honourably in the sight of God only by death.

Our society is having youth problems because marriage is not given validation, and divorce disapproval. The devil lies that there is "no-fault divorce", but the Bible says, "For I hate divorce!" says the Lord, the God of Israel." It is as cruel as putting on a victim's bloodstained coat," says the Lord Almighty, "So guard yourself; always remain loyal to your wife."(Malachi 2:16.) Let every husband and wife stand up and fight for their marriage.

It is worth fighting for, because many things depend on it, so fight for your home. Do not just quit because Quitters never win. Start from today to believe every Word of God for your marriage. I pray that, "your wife will be like a fruitful vine, flourishing within your home." (Psalm 128:8.) Don't believe what the enemy says; believe the Word of God.

Many times, we think there is nobody to pour our hearts out to; no mother to look after the kids, no one to give us the support or freedom that may be all we need to keep our marriage on track. Listen, I have been there, done it, bought the T-shirt. May I encourage you to search the Word of God (THE BIBLE) daily? Look for passages that talk on the area of your short comings. Start believing, meditating and practicing what the Word of God says about living a successful marital lifestyle. If you have to go for marriage counseling, to save your marriage, it worth every second of it, go for it. Buy books on successful marital relationships and read them and be master over your marital situations. Along the way, you will realize where the problem is, admit this weakness to God and be ready for a change.

I believe that one of the greatest and most comprehensive promises and revelations of God in scripture is when the Lord met Balaam and put a word of prophecy in his mouth and sending him to prophesy before Balak saying, "God is not a man that He should lie! He is not a human,

that He should change his mind. Has He ever spoken and failed to act?
Has He ever promise and not carried it through?" (Number 3:19.) Truly
God is not a man but a Spirit being, as taught by Jesus. As people that still
believe in the complete home that God created, i.e. (husband and wife)!
May I encourage you to read the Bible more with understanding and pray
for more wisdom, more endurance, patience, strength, tolerance and the
skills of marriage?

I believe you would love to have a golden wedding anniversary and a
big family gathering. Then from now on, pray more for your marriage, your
spouse and your children and that God will increase and strengthen your
tolerance and make your expectation not to be too high to cope with. One
of the reasons of writing this book is to let people realize the consequences
of people living together without getting married, i.e. the repercussions of
cohabitation.

You have to search yourself and be truthful; cohabitation is just a
modern self-indulgent non-solution to an eternal challenge. It promises
nothing good and it delivers nothing better. It is very common in the some
society. The living together of a man and a woman without getting married
is an undeniable foundation for conditional love, and conditional love is
not love, it is only a temporary permanence.

I pray as you read this book; that the Holy Spirit will help you and
inspire you with proper desires to fulfill the will of God for your marriage
in Jesus name. Amen. Get your spirit tuned into the will of God for your
marriage and I believe the Word of God that says, "Now to Him who, by
in consequence of the action of His power that is at work within us, is able
to carry out His purpose and do superabundantly, far over and above all
that we dare ask or think infinitely beyond our highest prayers, desires,
thoughts, hopes, or dreams."(Ephesians 3:20.)

I want you to understand that the small details of your lives are what
really matter in a relationship. It is not the mansion, the car, property, the
money in the bank. These create an environment conducive for happiness
but cannot give happiness in them self, so find time to be your spouse's
friend and do those little things for each other that build intimacy. I pray
that this book will be a blessing to you so that you can have a real happy
marriage in Jesus name!

Every married man has to support his wife and honour her for
undertaking the least thankless job in the world. When God wants to bless
a good man, He blesses him with a good wife. Your wife who was once a
young bride; will one day become a mother and from a mother to your

wonderful life partner. If you, as the husband will support, love and honour your wife's hard work, it will be a *marriage, a miracle of completion.* You can take a step of faith today for change to better marital lifestyle. I believe God want to receive glory in your marriage if you allow Him.

Begin now.

Let's pray,

"Heavenly Father, forgive us for not understanding your heart concerning marriage when you have made it clear in the scriptures. As I read this book and the scriptures, may I receive impartation, wisdom and revelation knowledge in the power of the Holy Spirit and the truth in the Word of God to have successful marital life? Lord Jesus, rain down on me pure, heaven born possibilities that have their foundation in the Holy Spirit, in Jesus name." Amen.

Let me encourage you to make a difference in your marital life with the people who make a difference that makes a difference in marital journey in this generation.

I BELIEVE

The original plan of God for marriage will never be broken no matter what the devil devises to break-up families.

CHAPTER 1

What You Must Know About Marriage

Marriage can be defined as memories and I pray in Jesus name that your marriage memories will be of joy and fulfillment, not of pain and heartbreaks. Amen. Hear what the scripture says, "Finally brothers whatever is true, whatever is right, whatever is pure, whatever is lovely, whatever is admirable—If anything is excellent or praiseworthy—think about such things." (Philippians 4:8.) Everyone that believes in God must live in Christian virtues and meditate on certain thing, but do certain things also. Christianity is very practical and there are things to practice and enjoy i.e. Things learned—Christian practices: Things received—Christian blessings: Things heard—Christian blessings: Things seen—Christian miracles. Truth be told, Christianity is not a dead, dry formal, human religion of rituals, outward form, and show, but a divine, living, vital, dynamic, liberating religion. One without power to deliver men from sin, sickness, poverty, and want, now and hereafter, is not of God.

Marriage is good and that is why the Bible says, "He who find a true wife finds a good thing and obtains favour from the Lord" (Proverb 18:22.) Who do you believe? Is it the True God or the modernization deception? For me, I believe GOD. Hear this, "By no means 'Let God be found true and every human being is false and a liar, as it is written, That you may be justified and shown to be upright in what you say, and prevail when you are judged."(Romans 3:4.) Let no man say that God has failed in keeping His Word with any man. Let man examine himself and his ways to see if he has not failed to meet conditions so God can fulfill His promise. May I encourage you to stand firm in your faith in God and eradicate the "We are technologically superior, more intelligent, and more independent self—talk we have been allowing this so called modern world culture to lie to us than believing the true word of God." Being technologically superior to the generations before us does not erase our yarning for the mystery of love affairs, does it?

You have to understand the reason why the Bible says, "The thief cometh not, but to steal and to kill and to destroy: I come that they might have life, and that they might have it more abundantly." (John 10:10.) The devil is the thief to steal, kill, and destroy but Jesus come that men might have abundant life. Every husband and wife should realize that marriage destruction could be internal or external. Internal forces will create a deep suspicion in both spouse and he or she will develop an intense hatred for the partner. This internal force can be in form of the spirit of anger.

The internal force can also appear in the form of lack of enough financial means in the home and this works against peace and unity in the home. Selfishness and unbroken spirit, arrogance in the life of either spouse can cause division in the home. This is why couples have to pray for deliverance from the destruction of their marriage. Satan is the enemy of man since the world began and he unleashes destruction on marriage and homes with the view of exterminating the human race. The devil is a liar.

As for external forces that couples should be aware of, they include household wickedness, demonic in-laws, and unfriendly friends. The Bible says "Woe to you, O destroyer, you who were not yourself destroyed, who deal treacherously though they (your victims) did not deal treacherously with you! When you have ceased to destroy, you will be destroyed; and when you have stopped dealing treacherously, they will deal treacherously with you." (Isaiah 33:1.) Husband and wife should be aware of Satan's plan in homes with conflicts and hostilities, as this is a very common phenomenon in this so-called modern day. "Can two walk together, except they are agreed?" (Amos 3:3.)

Husband and wife should try as much as possible to live in peace and be in agreement if they do not want Satan's strategy of disagreement and resentment to tear them apart. It is important to note and comply with what the Bible says that, "Do not let the sun go down upon your wrath". (Ephesians 4:26.) I know that it is not easy to do, but trust me, I have been there. If you love your spouse, your children and you do not want the curse of divorce on them, you have to think deeply and see that the benefit of peace in your home is far greater and better than getting angry, frustrated and bitter towards your spouse.

Anytime husband and wife do not settle their differences in time, it will allow an invisible barrier to come *in-between* them. This will break the wall of protections around your home and will also open the door for the enemy of marriage to strike. God wants you and me to have a perfect marriage but each marriage has its own challenges. You have to focus your marriage on God, and choose at all times the path of love and be spiritually matured to quickly resolve challenges or differences as it occur. This will help you build your home and relationship on the right path.

Husband and wife that do not resolve their differences in time will have conflicts and hostility in their home and this is what the Devil wants. Hear what the Bible says, "Two are better than one, because they have a good (more satisfying) reward for their labour: For if they fall, the one will lift up his fellow. But woe to him who is alone when he falls and has not another to lift him up! Again, if two lie down together, then they have warmth; but how can one be warm alone? And though a man might prevail against him who is alone, two will withstand him. A threefold cord is not quickly broken."(Ecclesiastes 4:9-12.)

Husband and wife should realize that two are better than one and this is to their advantage. You and your spouse have more reward for your labour: One can lift the other one up if he falls: Both can keep warm: You and your spouse can prevail against another. There is more power when people pray in unity. But you should be aware that Satan would try all his tricks to cause conflicts and hostilities between couples so that they do not agree on anything and so that they do not pray together.

Every husband and wife must remember that Satan is on the lookout for loopholes to strike especially in time of weakness and disobedience to God. In obedience to God, the children of Israel would have never been defeated. God had sold them to go into defeat and captivity, and shut them up because of their disobedient. "How could one have chased a thousand, and two put ten thousand to flight, except their Rock had sold them, and the Lord had delivered them up?" (Deuteronomy 32:30.)

Marriage is just like the shape of a triangle. We have God at the top, the husband and the wife at the bottom. This signifies that God is the one holding the marriage together. Husband and wife must not neglect the family altar so that the enemy of marriage will not have a foothold in their home. Another strategy which the enemy can use against marriage is the spirit misunderstanding and confusion, which disrupts the free flow of God's power and blessings in the home.

I want you to honestly ask yourself why things are not going on well in your home. Or why you are still have misunderstanding in your marriage after you have tried everything. Furthermore, you must to understand that there are negative forces operatives being busy planning and working to scatter Christian homes and destroy their marriages. The aim of these forces is not to your advantage, as it will ultimately bring about separation and divorce. At this stage, you should take care of the situation with prayer and fasting. I mean serious prayer, fasting, and marriage counseling if need be. The Bible says that, "For this reason a man shall leave (behind) his father and his mother and be joined to his wife and cleave closely to her permanently. And the two shall become one flesh, so that they are no longer two, but one flesh. What therefore God has united (joined together), let not man separated or divide." (Mark 10:7-9.)

I pray that the Lord will give you the wisdom knowledge and understanding of marriage institution so that you do not abuse it and seek divorce in Jesus name. Anyone that does not understand the purpose of a thing tends to abuse it. Divorce is an abuse; a disgraceful and shameful act as far as the institution of marriage is concerned. These are some of the things God commanded us to do as a guide line to have a good marital lifestyle:

(a) A man must leave his father and his mother to form a relationship with his wife i.e. (a covenant with his wife.)
(b) The Bible says that the husband and wife should *cleave* together and become one flesh.
(c) The couple should accept each other, for better or worse, till death separates them. They should stay together through thick and thin. I believe that God makes no provision for divorce in His master plan.

Married couples must understand that negative forces responsible for breaking up families is hovering around like hawks, looking for a prey. Apostle Peter said, "Be well balanced, be vigilant and cautious at all times for that enemy of yours, the devil, roams around like a lion roaring in fierce hunger, seeking someone to seize upon and devour."(I Peter 5:8.) Every husband and wife must understand that the basic building block for homes and marriages is love. This love or the lack of it, will affect your health, physical and spiritual wellbeing in general and that of your spouse including your children in either positive or negative way. May I suggest that you start affirming your love to your spouse from today and frequently by saying, "I LOVE YOU?" It goes a long way to remind one another of this love as an assurance that no matter what, you are there for each other. I believe love feeds on love, and the more love you give, the more it bounces back.

Everyone has an idea of what a home is and how it should be but many of us are limited on how to make things work positively to both husband and wife. It is clear that it is not just a matter of co-habiting for a man and a woman to come together to build a home. Each person comes into this relationship with his own individual personality traits, joined together on a mutual terrain. The goal of this union is for the couple to spend the rest of their lives together, creating a warm, happy and safe environment. The two individuals have different tastes, attitudes and backgrounds. Any attempt by one of the couple to force the partner to become a replica of him or her is a recipe for a bitter end to the marriage.

I believe the differences in the physical, emotional and psychological make-up of the two people, (male and female) could make their marriage stronger if well harnessed. If one member of the couple is shy and finds it difficult to mix with people but the other member is an extrovert who easily connects with others, this will help them as a couple, to complement one another. The husband or the wife may be good at organizing things while the other partner is rather good at handling technical things. Each person will bring to the marriage what the other partner lacks and this will complement the marriage to grow from strength to strength and help the couple to find fulfillment and joy.

Each partner should develop the habit of honouring and showing respect for one another day by day. You should remind one another of your love and the following type of expression should be frequently heard: "I couldn't be what I am without your love, help and support. I do appreciate you always, I thank you" If you can love yourself and see your own good qualities, then you can switch the focus on to your partner and acknowledge his or her worth even in better terms than how you see yourself. The lack of these had made many young people unhappy and is always on the defensive. They argue unnecessarily with their parents at home because they are growing up in an unhappy environment. There is tension and stress everywhere and this situation is manifesting more and more in the home, which is the centre of a child's world.

So when such child grows up to get married, they go into their own marital life with the baggage of unhappy environment from their parents, creating such atmosphere like their parents. I want every parent to understand that their children are observing how they communicate and treat one another. The verbal behaviour of parent to one another forms the foundation of the communication skills for their children and this is why children often repeat the words they hear from their parents, and often with the same tone. The building of a good relationship of parent will give their children a happy and bright future to achieve their potentials to succeed in life.

To be a better parent especially when talking to your children, you should try as much as possible to use precise language and say exactly what you mean and avoid shouting. When this is done, your children will realize that they must listen at all times to what their parent say and are serious about it. As a parent, you should let your children see that you listen to them too by giving attention, affection and appreciation. By this, your children will not feel neglected and start to be rebellious. You should try not to make a promise that you cannot keep, and if these happened you should apologize and let them see the reason why what you promised cannot be achieve. Broken promises bring children to distrust their parents and everything should be done to avoid this ugly situation.

Husband and wife should be ready to dig deep in constantly in assessing their marriage situation at every point in time so that they can move from anger and hurt to forgiveness and renewal. Each partner must be willing to re-commit and restore trust and confidence in one another anytime there is a challenge in their marriage. Every good marriage is built on the foundation of trust and honesty. If each member of the couple is steadfast through trying periods, they will grow and be strengthened together.

If you are experiencing challenges in your marriage now, may I encourage you to fight for your marriage because if you do, you have a good chance of winning? Do not give up on your marriage because God did not give up on you. God hates divorce, and you should understand this. Truth be told, if you want your partner to change, you should change yourself first. A marriage is more than just a simple commitment to a person: it is a complex web of relationships, shared memories and experiences. This is more than just meeting your needs. It is about creating a family and doing those small daily acts of kindness that say "I LOVE YOU" to your spouse.

This is a tough world and we have to be persistent. Quitting your marriage is giving in to frustration. Do not turn back, rather accept the frustration as a challenge and work on it till you find a solution. Do not allow your problems to harass you, but rather solve it. The truth is, you cannot make anyone to love you and nobody can make you happy except God. May I encourage you to do His will daily, and you will be connected to eternity. It's important that you understand not to try to change your spouse, however, if you change yourself, your spouse may change.

Nowadays, people do not marry real people, but marry illusions and fantasies. That is the whole truth which many people do not want to hear. And remember that your spouse is as human as you are. Believe it or not, real marriage begins just at the point where the illusion ends. The first challenge for any newly married couples is that, you must discover who you are married to, and the reality of love is one of the reasons why you must choose your life partner correctly.

May I encourage you today as a married man or woman, to take a memory lane and think back to those old days when you first met your spouse? It is likely that the qualities that now drive you mad are the same ones that first attracted you to your spouse. You should remember the saying: "no pain, no gain". It is impossible to go through a relationship without experiencing period of pain and loneliness for a short period but it will surely come one day. I believe the greatest gift you can give your children as a parent is a loving and peaceful environment to grow. You need to realize this before it is too late that the needs of your spouse are as important as yours for a successful marriage. The marital relationship offers the best opportunity to grow and overcome selfishness and learn to grow love.

Couples that want to have a successful marriage need to be committed to the goals of giving each other pleasure. By staying together and being focused on the most important goal, which is to give to one another love and not pain. Then, this will eventually bring God blessings upon both of you. This encouragement may sound simple but I know it is hard to implement, but you can start one day at a time to put it into practice. Every married person must ask himself or herself this question daily: "Will what I am about to do or say cause my spouse pain or pleasure?" This is better than mind reading and I believe when you put it into practice, lot of arguments will be avoided.

Let me advice you to avoid at all cost anything in your relationship that would get to the level of abusing one another, where a partner is afraid to express his or her feelings and opinions. Husband and wife must create a conducive and safe environment that allows each partner to feel comfortable to express freely his or her mind. This should be the building block that husband and wife can express anything that bothers them so that understanding and peace can be attained as soon as it is practicable.

Let me share with you a good communication skill to resolve hostile situation. It is called the "Listener-Speaker Technique". Many couples try to find a solution before giving their partner the chance to say what he or she wants to communicate. The Speaker-Listener Technique works very well in that it allows both husband and wife in the solution talk and gives each partner the feeling that each one has been fully heard. It is a good habit for husband and wife to constantly turn towards each other instead of turning away from one another.

For example, if your spouse is sitting at a desk doing some work, do stop by her and rub her shoulders or give him or her kiss on the cheek or whisper something nice to him or her. Do not just walk away or walk by. You see, happily married couples do a lot of turning towards each other whenever they get the opportunity. Husband and wife should always look out for opportunities to be physically and emotionally close to each other. The little bits and pieces are more important than many married couples have realized that can make their marriage more productive. Believe it or not, the true test for any marriage is in all the tiny opportunities to give or not to give your best to your spouse.

Your dedication to your spouse will really be tested when you are tired, distracted, frustrated or under pressure with coping with life's daily challenges. In those periods, you need to put your spouse interest first above your own. You must realize that your marriage depends for success on your positive actions and you need to try as much as possible to use the right and appropriate words that suit positive actions. May I encourage you to make up your mind and determine to believe every Word of God (i.e. The Bible) concerning your marriage? Hear this, "He whose deeds exceed his wisdom, his wisdom shall endure; but he whose wisdom exceeds his deeds, his wisdom shall not endure."

Additionally "He whose wisdom exceeds his deeds,—what does he resembles? A tree with many boughs and few roots: Winds, springing up, uproot it, and overturn it. But he whose deeds exceed his wisdom—what does he resemble? A tree with few boughs but many roots: Though all the winds in the world come and blow at it, it cannot be budged." The same is true of marriage and the truth of the whole matter is that another person cannot make your marriage work. It is your own responsibility to make it work better.

Husband and wife need "meaningful time" just like human beings needs water to survive. The reason for any husband and wife that wants to be happy in their marital life is to enrich their relationship by sharing meaningful experiences with one another. And it is one of the reasons that married couples should study the Word of God (the Bible) together. It may not be practicable every day, but it should be done at every available opportunity. This will lead to an establishment of a common philosophy of life as well as that of a common physical and spiritual life-purpose.

I know it may be hard to do but if you put your mind to it and with the help of the Holy Spirit you will accomplish your aim. Start to believe the Word of God from today for the Bible says that, "I can do all things through Jesus Christ that strengthens me" (Philippians 4:13.) I want you to understand that you can share truly and meaningful experiences together with your spouse and operate on a deeper level than you can imagine. This may appear to be difficult to achieve at first, but when practice consistently; it will form the backbone of your successful and fulfilling marital life.

Hear this analysis of a last born male in a family married to a first born female of another family. There is always conflict in their home until they realize what the problem was and a balance was reached. The analyst realize that every last born male in every family is always expecting things to be done for him, because he is used to his siblings getting things done for him. Likewise majority of first born female child in her family is always a goal getter. She is the one to help her mother in the kitchen, look after her junior ones.

So she is used to be caring for others. She is the first child that was born when mum and dad are still struggling to see how the marriage will work out. Now that she is old enough to get married, she will be expecting her husband to be like her; a goal getter. Unfortunately, things may not work out that way for the couple due to their upbringing that is different completely. I believe many husband and wife can relate to this, and use this piece of wisdom to complement one another.

May I encourage any husband or wife that may think of changing their spouse lifestyle, to have the second thought that you can only change yourself not the other way round? Let me advice you that the earlier you stop comparing your spouse to other people, the better things will be, because each person is unique in the sight of God. Another area that may be causing misunderstanding in the home is the upbringing of the middle child whether male or female. When they get married, they still want to live the life style of, "Nobody care or listen to me mentality".

Majority of middle child has the mentality from their childhood that nobody cares for them. Dad or mum doesn't always listen to them at home. May I suggest to any middle child reading this book that is not yet married that may realize this situation before getting married to change their "nobody care about me" mentality so that you may have a good marital life. Bur if you can handle these situation and have a good understanding of one another weakness to strike out balance, so be it and have a good and successful marital life.

Let me encourage you as a married woman to move you to the level of matured Christian woman that the Bible talked about, of how the women should conduct themselves. "For it was thus that the pious women of old who hoped in God were (accustomed) to beautify themselves and were submissive to their husbands (adapting themselves to them as themselves secondary and dependent upon them). It was thus that Sarah obeyed Abraham (following his guidance and acknowledging his headship over her by) calling him lord (master, leader, authority). And you are now her true daughters if you do right and let nothing terrify you (not giving way to hysterical fears or letting anxieties unnerve you). In the same way you married men should live considerately with (your wives) with and intelligent recognition (of the marriage relation), honouring the woman as (physically) the weaker, but (realizing that you) are joint heirs of the grace (God's unmerited favour) of life, in order that your prayers may not be hindered and cut off. (Otherwise you cannot pray effectively.)" (1 Peter 3:5-7.)

May I pray this prayer with you?

"Heavenly Father, forgive me for not believing and obeying your Word as I ought to. As I read your Word from today, may I receive your truth with understanding that will set me free from whatever bondage I may have put myself? Holy Spirit, help me to recognize my spouse as my divine assignment to love and celebrate always. Teach me to use my tongue right, so that I may use it as a blessing tool to my spouse and other people always. Lord Jesus, teach me to know what to say to you every day so that I may experience the joy of marriage that brings deeper joy and happiness that comes with fulfilling my potentials in Jesus name. Teach me to number my days that I may apply my heart to wisdom daily. All this, I ask in Jesus mighty name!" Amen.

CHAPTER 2

The Marriage Institution

The lasting marriage is never sure of the separate "selves" that make it up. But it has complete confidence in God that the relationship will grow in a never-ending process of learning. The Bible says that I can do all things through Christ who strengthens me. (Philippians 4:13.) I believe the Bible confession is a very powerful healing force of God for love. The best way to have a lasting love is to pray for the anointing type of God-love, sense it, send it and make it grow. You can not do this by yourself unless through the power of the Holy Spirit through Jesus Christ.

You will be energized in your relationship with your spouse when you put your trust in God and do not lean on your own understanding. "Lean on, trust in, and be confident in the Lord with all your heart and mind and do not rely on your own insight or understanding. In all your ways know, recognize, and acknowledge Him and He will direct and make straight and plain your path." (Proverbs 3:5-6). Negative energy comes from conflict that arise when two egos collide. That is why husband and wife should avoid foolish arguments, and grow up to start loving again. It is better to learn to love than to fight and you should not try to win for yourself but should win for your marriage.

God designed marriage as an avenue to love, to give rather than to receive. Every husband that wants to succeed in their marriage should always remember the Word of God that says, He is acting as the witness between you and the wife of your youth because you have broken faith with her, though she is your partner, the wife of your marriage covenant. (Malachi 2:14) As far as God is concerned, marriage should be a permanent union of two unselfish people. "For the Lord, the God of Israel says; I hate divorce and marital separation and him who cover his garment (his wife) with violence. Therefore keep a watch upon your spirit (that it may be controlled by My Spirit), that you deal not treacherously and faithlessly (with your marriage mate)." (Malachi 2:16) So every husband should guide against breaking faith.

When Jesus was asked if it is lawful to divorce one's wife for any and every reason? "He replied. Have you never read that He who made them from the beginning made them male and female? And said, for this reason a man shall leave his father and mother and shall be united firmly (joined inseparably) to his wife, and two shall become one flesh? So they are no longer two, but one flesh. What therefore God has joined together let not man put asunder (separate)." (Matthew 19: 4-6).

The Word of God says that marriage should be honoured by all and the marriage bed kept pure, for God will judge the adulterers and all those who are sexually immoral. (Hebrew 13: 5).

Let every man have his own wife.

Let every woman have her own husband.

Let the husband meet the sexual needs of the wife and let the wife meet the sexual needs of her husband. I want you to understand the thing that makes sex powerful in marriage is the celebration of that which was once joined together, then separated, coming back together again. It is the celebration of what we are before. I certainly understand why God tells the wife to be in submission to her own husband as unto the Lord. He tells the husband to love his wife as Christ love the Church. This is a commandment from God to every married man and woman, to obey and follow. There is no negotiation, and anything less of what God says is disobedient to Him.

Let me put it straight to challenge you as a married couple that you has been typecast to play a part in marital relationship. Your role as the husband is to play Christ, and your wife is to play the Church. So when God plant you in the neighborhood that doesn't understand what the Bible is saying about marriage! I believe your marriage should dramatize your relationship between Christ and the Church. That is why husband and wife have to pray together, read together, make decision together and continue dating one another again and again. I can understand that falling has seemed effortless, but building your marriage and keeping it strong does require hard work. However the blessing, joy and reward of that effort are priceless and immeasurable.

The husband should not defraud his wife and the wife must not defraud her husband. Each one should respect their marriage vow. Come together again after you have consented to abstain from sexual relationship for a period to fast and pray. A wife should not depart from her husband and if she does, she should remain alone or be reconciled back to her husband according to the Word of God in; (I Cor. 7:11). The husband should not divorce his wife and a Christian husband must not divorce his non-Christian wife if she wants to remain with him. If the un-believer husband or wife wants to get out of the marriage with a Christian, he or she is free to get out. No one should force the continuance of the marriage. The Christian is free from the marriage bond in such a case. Everyone should remain as they were when they became a Christian. Christianity should not be used as an excuse to break a marriage, and perhaps to seek a new companion.

If you are bound to a wife, seek not to be loosed by getting a divorce regardless of what may have happened in the past. Stay in the same marital status in which you were when you were saved. If you were loosed from a wife, seek not another wife but if you do marry, you have not sinned. If you are married, live as though you have no wife, free from all anxiety. Married Christians are bound by the laws of God to remain married as long as both partners are alive. Marriage is for the lifetime of the husband and wife. If one of the married partners dies, and the partner desires to re-marry, God expects the man or the woman to marry a Christian. (I Cor. 7:39).

The Bible says that a husband should be just and faithful to his wife as he wants her to do to him. He should not give his wife any excuse for sin. (1 Peter 3:7). He should give honour to his wife, using his strength to protect her because you and your wife are co-heirs of life. Husband and wife should care very much for one another as many prayers are hindered because of their unfaithfulness as married couple. Christian couple should be of one mind according to (1 Peter 3:8), and (Eph. 4:1-3).

Husband and wife should have compassion on one another and love each other as brethren. They should be tender hearted and courteous to one another. There should be no returning of evil for evil between husband and wife and both of you should be source of blessing to each other. To have a good marriage, both husband and wife must have control over their tongues. The Bible warns us that he that loves life and wants to see good days should caution his tongue from evil and his lips from spreading bitterness. (I Peter 3:10).

Husband and wife must learn to manifest forgiveness, meekness, gentleness and complete self-control that Christ teaches. It may be difficult to achieve this by human ability, but with God all things are possible. You need to pray about every situation and call the Holy Spirit to intervene on your behalf. The Word of God makes it clear that says, you can do all things through Christ who strengthens you. (Philippians 4:13) Amen. The Holy Spirit filled family head should pray for spiritual power in the inner man and the indwelling of Jesus Christ so as to be deeply rooted in Christ and in His love. He should pray for spiritual understanding concerning all the affairs of his family and be rooted in love.

Apostle Paul wrote to the Corinthians churches that the body is for the Lord, not for fornication and sin. He said, "You may say, "Food is for the stomach, and the stomach is for the food." This is true, though someday God will do away with both of them. But our bodies were not made for sexual immorality. They were made for the Lord, and the Lord cares about our bodies." (I Corinthians 6:13). God has made appetite for food and food for appetite, yet He has not made the body for immoral acts, but for the Lord. I believe that you understand that all sins destroy, but he who commits fornication sins against his entire constitution, even his body, soul and spirit.

"Flee fornication, every sin that a man doeth is without the body, but he that committed fornication commits against his own body". (1 Corinthians 6:18) The body must be free from sin as the temple of God. I want you to understand that not every man or woman is required to be married, but those who choose to be are permitted by Christianity to get married. Then husband and wife must respect one another regarding lawful sexual needs; pay the matrimonial debt and render the conjugal duty to each other, mutually satisfying each other. Any husband or wife who does not obey this injunction may be responsible for the infidelity of his or her spouse. Husband and wife belong to one another. May I say that, either of you has any authority to refuse what the other needs or demands in normal, temperate relationship. All acts of perversion or unnatural affection must absolutely reject.

Husband and wife must not deny one another their marital duty except by mutual consent for a time agreed upon for fasting and praying. Then, regardless of the spiritual blessing either one has received, should come together again to defeat Satan. Remember this that your spouse is your assignment, your ministry, your helpmeet, your spiritual song in the night, your do you right. Hear me clearly right now, that the perception you have for him or her will affects your marriage either negative or positive. You need the right perception towards your spouse to enjoy your marital life to the full, or you will lose him or her to someone else that has the right perceptive.

Let's pray!

Holy Spirit, I welcome you in our home. Reveal to me the secret of our marital success that is hidden in our daily routine. Lord, teach me your statues and the way of your statues. Teach me good judgment and knowledge so that I can do your will daily, in Jesus name. Amen.

CHAPTER 3

The True Meaning of Love

One basic definition of love as a verb is "to value or cherish". Love is an active emotion and the act of demonstrating value and looking for the good of another person.

One can say:

L—Is for listening. To love someone is to listen without any condition to his value, logic and needs without prejudice.

O—Is for overlook. To love someone is to overlook the flaws and the faults in favor of looking for the good.

V—Is for voice. To love someone is to voice your approval of him on a regular basis. There is no substitute for honest encouragement and positive strokes and praise.

E—Is for effort. To love someone is to make a constant effort to spend time with that person or make the sacrifice and go an extra mile to show your interest.

The truth is that you have to love yourself first before you can give that love to somebody else. Loving requires independence and is based on the ability to share oneself with others out of choice, not out of dependent need. True love is the relationship formed by two individuals who have the ability of independently supporting themselves.

The representation of the modern wife may not be the best that God want. The modern wife is portrayed as a latex concept that can stretch to any dimension to cover all eventualities. A wife these days can work if she wants to and there is nothing bad in that but there should be a limit. A wife responsibility is to make sure she prepares and feeds her family well and not fill them with junk food from the fast food shops. The idea that a modern wife can choose not to ruin her figure by not having children is not acceptable because this is one of the reasons that God instituted marriage. If there are no health problems or impediment, it is expected that every wife should have their own children and be a loving mother.

A good wife of noble character, who can find? She is worth far more that what money can buy. The husband has full confidence in her and lacks nothing of value. She brings the husband good, not harm all the days of her life. She opens her hand to the poor and needy. This is what is called the love that last and to have this experience in marriage, you need to rekindle your relationship again and again. That means dating should not stop in your marriage, but as means of keeping the flame alive. Wait a minute, rewind your memory tape and visualize the first date with your spouse. You can say those are the good old days but you know what? Those times like that can also be brought back if you are ready to work on it and it will be more real than before.

The truth is, you can recapture the best aspect of dating experience in your marriage now as before; the romance, the surprise, the fun, the undivided attention etc. You know what, this is real and things will be a little different this time around. One of the best parts of dating in marriage is that the person you will be dating will not care how much you may spend. He or she is used to you and loves you anyway! You don't have to impress him or she like the first time, but just being with you alone is a pleasure and a treat. He or she has already seen you at your best times and at your worst and still loves you anyway. You know what? Who wouldn't want to date this person; of course this person is your spouse. Your mate for life and that person has made a marriage covenant with you and wants to keep it till death do you part. That man or woman has lived with you through the good times and the bad times. He or she knows you inside out and still love you.

Bear in mind that, the person has being with you before the kid and through the kids and want to have special time alone with you. Wow, dating your husband or wife again and again rejuvenates your marriage and it is very different from dating a potential spouse. Even though you have been husband and wife for some time but I still believe that you need to love one another like the first time you met. You still need to rekindle your love to one another frequently. Both of you has to feel more passionate and at ease with each other as you face new challenges; create time to talk together alone to discuss your dream for the future. This is one of the reasons why Dating your spouse shouldn't stop in marriage. It doesn't matter how long you've been married and it is not too late to get into the habit of dating your spouse again and again.

I know that one of you may come up with different excuses about time and money. If you love your wife or your husband as you love yourself, then create the time and save for the date, but not too expensive. May I encourage as a good husband or wife that wants to have a fantastic and successful marital life to reconnect your love frequently and fan the romance in your marriage everyday. You can start by calling your spouse at work to check her welfare, or going to movie or dinner alone together without the children around! You can start by even just having a walk with her alone in the evening or jugging together. All these bits and pieces of things you normally do together before you got married can be done again.

Marriage in the Bible is symbolic of the relationship between Jesus Christ and the believers. The Church is the bride of Jesus Christ. Jesus as the bridegroom is coming to take the bride away. A man and woman stand in the presence of God and people to make a vow to each other by word, and then the veil is lifted. This is the picture of Jesus Christ who will come to lift the veil and simple man is taken away. One thing is certain, if anyone accepts Jesus Christ as the Lord and Saviour, the veil will be lifted and the person will become the bride of Christ.

To build a marriage that will last, husband and wife need to study how Rebecca took Sarah's place. For a Christian marriage, husband and wife need to see their relationship as very important, not because of your children, your friends or your parents but because both of you love each other as God commanded you to do. Husband and wife should honour one another by attaching high value to your relationship; to treat each other as a priceless treasure in your life and this will make you build a solid healthy relationship.

Love is not a myth. You have to be deeply committed to the relationship to benefit from it and to make that happen; a lot of investment in terms of efforts and time must be put into the relationship. One of the reasons why marriages break up easily is the lack of total commitment. Many people just want the easy ride but you should realize that what anyone can easily achieved in most of the time is not worth fighting to keep. A good and loving marriage needs a lot of work. You must be patient and you should not try to force your partner to change to what you want but first work on yourself to have a self-change. In marriage, a lot is given and a lot is demanded if you want the benefits of a good relationship.

As I've already said, successful marriage demands a lot of effort and time to make it happen. We can imagine marriage as a marathon race that demands great preparation and discipline. A daily training that aims at completing the race must be followed. You have to train for success in marriage by working on your communication skills, learning to give to your partner, building trust, expressing your love in words and deed most of the time. I am confident that anyone that practiced all these qualities daily has what is lacking in many marriages today, i.e. (happiness and joy.)

To have happiness and joy in marriage, you have to love and be loved. Love is the constant choice of giving the best to the other person. You have to create and fall in love with your spouse again and again, lovingly giving yourself to him or her more. When one functions as a giver, love is created. The more a man or a woman invests in anything or anybody, the more attached him/she would be to that thing or person. Many people has a wrong mentality concerning their relationship by waiting or looking for what their partner can do for them but not what they can do for their partner. This is a negative approach to have a successful marital life.

Let me encourage every husband to arise as God has ordained from the beginning. God made you the head of your home and not the tail. You have to affirm and understood this authority God has place on you. Whatever the situation or the situation in your home, do not lose your headship and your God given authority. It goes a long way than the physical aspect of family life. This is a spiritual authority over every husband that obey God commandment, to love his wife as Christ love the church.

Let me digress a little bit here. Even though, your wife brings home a bigger pay packet than you, it does not matter. As long as you are doing all that you can do, to bring money home as long as it is through legal means that is call a legitimate job. I can understand that many husbands have lost their job due to the world financial melt down, but I believe this is just temporary. That does not mean that you have lost your headship as the head of your home.

What the Word of God says about your headship as the husband is the final arbiter. God wanted a family, so he created Adam. Adam is lonely, so Eve was created. These are the chain of creation and remember this, God created man in His own image. In the image of God He created him, male and female He created them. (Genesis 1:27.) Hear these, "The Lord God placed the man in the Garden of Eden to tend and care for it. But the Lord God gave him this warning: "You may freely eat any fruit in the garden except fruit from the tree of knowledge of good and evil. If you eat of its fruit, you will surely die." And the Lord God said. "It is not good for the man to be alone. I will make a companion who will help him." (Genesis 2:16-18.) The truth is that God created and spoke to the man first before the woman was created.

God saw that His work was not yet completed in that man was not complete and could not reproduce his kind alone. So He made a help-meet for him to enable him to propagate his kind, i.e. (a help suitable to man intellectually, morally and physically.) The Bible says: "And out of the ground the Lord God formed every (wild) beast and living creature of the field and every bird of the air and brought them to Adam to see what he would call them; and whatever Adam called every living creature, that was its name." (Genesis 2:19) God did the first anesthesia and major operation on Adam to make a woman, (Eve.)

I believe that if you want to have a happy marriage, intimacy must be protected against any and all intrusion by impenetrable barriers. Husband and wife must remind themselves that frequent communion is important to have a healthy relationship. It should be made clear to everyone that your marriage is unique and out of bounds to anyone else. Everyone must understand that the physical and emotionally aspect of marital relationship is not for sharing with anyone outside of the marriage. The intensity of the intimacy of marriage must not be weakened nor is its wall broken to allow any intruder. Husband and wife must realize that anytime either of them connect physically with anyone of the opposite gender outside marriage, is opening a crack in the wall of their marriage intimacy. The problem is that it will create distance between you and your spouse.

Husband and wife must know the potential risks in their marriage if a narrow opening occurs in their amour. Care must be taken to build a protective and impenetrable wall around marriage intimacy. No inappropriate relationship must be allowed to come in-between the married couple. If it has happened in your life and you don't want a re-occurrence of such a thing in the life of your children when they become married in the near future, then, deal with the issues now before it is too late. Be a good example to your children positively.

Husband, always encourages yourself in the Word of God as the real man that God wants you to be. You must wake up and be what God ordained you to be, not as the world or the society thinks that you should be. You are the head of your home as Christ is the head of the Church. You must always remind yourself that you must love your wife and be kind to her, appreciate her and express it more often. You must not belittle your wife in any way or attack people that are dear to her. Peace in the home is not the exclusive responsibility of the wife alone but the joint responsibility of both husband and wife. Husband and wife must pray constantly for Godly wisdom to help them grow in love. Every husband that wants a good marital life must not underestimate the power of small gestures, special smile, a little note, a small gift and a loving word because this always goes a long way.

Both husband and wife should always remember that the secret of a strong marriage is for each partner to focus on giving to one another. The more each partner gives, the more their love will grow and respect one another at all times. Your actions, tone of voice, facial expression and words should all reflect commitment to relationship. You must not intimidate one another by shouting, stamping of feet, door slamming, blocking of passage, violating one another's space and breaking of things if you want to enjoy your marriage to the full. Married couples must always control their anger; especially the husband, to express himself in a non-threatening and non-destructive manner against his wife. Both husband and wife should let the rain of peace and love be in their home frequently so as to make it a place of respect, love, joy and harmony.

Married couples should always remember that Satan is on the lookout for your weak point to capitalize on your emotions by creating an opportunity for argument in your home. It may result to emotional stress, lack of joy because Satan is trying to distract your focus from what God has called you to be. May I encourage you that as soon as you notice any unusual happening in your marriage, you must engage in prayer and ask God for wisdom and His grace to deal with any situation that may want to cause misunderstanding in your home. Now you know who is at work to cause this problem. Then you need to step back, keep quiet when you're angry, so that you do not do or say things you may regret later. This is where every husband and wife that believes God should be careful not to fall prey to Satan tricks, because he goes to and fro, seeking for the home to destroy.

I want you to understand that when God wants to bless a man; He brings him a good woman to marry as his wife. You need to know that God hides His greatest treasure; it is only the wise that will find it. So let the Holy Spirit be in control of your marriage, so that you can start to enjoy your marital life to the full.

Godly wife confession!

I am a supportive wife, not the one to boss my husband around.
I am not a doormat wife but his helpmate.
I will follow his leadership with love not by force.
I am not a nagging or complaining wife.
I believe God is able to speak to my husband without me interfering.
All this I confess in Jesus name. Amen

CHAPTER 4

Illustration of the Difference
Between a Man and a Woman

There was once a businessman who was in the Navy in his youth days. Then, everyone referred to the ship with the pronoun "she". Upon retiring, he started his business and one day as he was working on his computer; he wondered what pronoun to use for his computer, a "she" or a "he"? He first called together his female staff and then his male staff to seek their opinion concerning this. The women thought that the computer should get the pronoun "he" because to get its attention, you have to turn it on and also because the computer is supposed to help you solve your problem but that after some time, it will become a problem itself. The women said that as soon as you commit yourself to one (a computer), you will realize that if you have waited a little bit longer, you could have got a better one.

The men said a computer should receive the pronoun "she" because only the initiated understands its internal logic and the language he uses to communicate with it is incomprehensible to everyone else. Even your smallest mistakes are stored in long-term memory. As soon as you make a commitment to one, (a computer) you will find yourself spending your pay packet on accessories. I want everyone to have the understanding that real marriage is a commitment. My prayer is that your marriage will be a success according to the master plan of God.

The good example of marriage in the Bible is that of Isaac and Rebecca. It is interesting that in our society today, if people have been married for some time, we honour them. Despite this, there are many things in our society today that really undermine marriage institution. For example, the media and the society generally glorify adultery and immorality as normal. The society allows divorce for almost any reason and very quick to separate husband and wife. We see many single people living together (co-habiting) and teenage girls getting pregnant, but in the end, everybody wishes marriage could last and commitment could hold together.

Many marriages fail because the couple does not understand one another and are selfish. We are at the generation of what we can get only from our spouse and not what we can give to our spouse. This is the generation of what have you done for me lately mindset and that is not the attitude we should have as husband and wife that wants to have a good marital life. The first thing we should do is to change our attitude to our spouse by changing our self if we want our spouse to change for the best. You should start to understand your spouse inadequacy so that you don't continue to live in anger, bitterness and getting upsetting every time.

May I encourage you to move to the level of understanding your spouse more than ever before by accepting he or she the way God made him or her to be and not by you trying to change your spouse to the way you want him or her to be? Your responsibility is not for you to change your spouse because you are not the porter; you are not your spouse creator. Hear this; your spouse doesn't have to be like you and that is the truth. You have to make allowance for your spouse and overlook some things so that you don't always lose your peace over small issues just because your spouse is not like you. Don't allow the devil to steal your joy by getting upset every time and losing your sleep because of your spouse weakness.

My prayer for you today is that God will show you His mercy and loving kindness to heal whatever area in your situation including marital life that needs healing in Jesus name. I want you to understand the covenant of marriage between a man and a woman being ordained by God. The true perfection of a covenant is to establish a relationship that is not easy to break by any contrary spirit. You must understand that marriage relationship is not entirely just for sex alone but with everything that comes with this institution as God ordained. You need the understanding that real marriage covenant does not start just when the couple goes to the altar, but it starts from the beginning of their courtship.

A man or woman should not get married solely on their feelings because feelings are not constant and if feelings change, the marriage may deteriorate and reach rock bottom. A marriage based on an everlasting covenant of God will surely succeed by His grace. Every married man or woman should be proud of their wedding band/ring, especially husbands because it is a symbol that one is committed to a partner for life and that one is no more available to others for this type of covenant relationship.

Hear this, "Has not the Lord made them one? In flesh and Spirit they are his. And why did God say "one"? This is because God is seeking for godly offspring. So one should be watchful in the spirit and guide against breaking faith with the wife of his youth. For the Lord, the God of Israel says; I hate divorce and marital separation and him, who, covers his garment (his wife) with violence. Therefore keep a watch upon your spirit (that it may be controlled by my spirit), that you deal not treacherously and faithlessly (with your marriage mate)." (Malachi 2:15-16.) One must be watchful in the spirit and should not break faith. When the marriage covenant is broken, people suffer including the children. The covenant of marriage offers the perfect mutual assistance to both husband and wife so that when one partner is weak or tired, the other will complement.

The Bible says," God created the man in his image; in the image of God He created him, male and female He created them." (Genesis 1:27.) God birth the first man, and called his name Adam without a woman in three parts, (body, soul and spirit.) There is something about God you need to understand. God is man enough to be the Father of creation and Mother enough to be the breasted one. He has everything within Himself. He is all sufficient. The first human was created as an androgynous being which gives us much more meaning into male-female relationship and this was before Eve is created. The Bible says, "Now the Lord God said, It is not good (sufficient, satisfactory) that the man should be alone; I will make him a help meet (suitable, adapted, complementary) for him." (Genesis 2:18)

Then God perform the first anesthetics and major operation on Adam to create Eve. The Bible says, "And the Lord God caused a deep sleep to fall upon Adam, and while he slept, He took one of his ribs or a part of his side and closed the (place with) flesh. And the rib or part of his side which the Lord God had taken from the man He built up and made into a woman, and He brought her to the man. Then Adam said this (creature) is now bone of my bones and flesh of my flesh; she shall be called Woman, because she was taken out of a man." (Genesis 2:21-23) It is literally mean that Eve is she-man; womb-man; man with the womb; or female-man, because she was taken out of man. You need to understand that a woman is said not to have been taken out of man's head to be lorded over by him, nor from his feet to be trampled on him, but from his side to be equal with him, from under his arm to be protected by him, and from near his heart to be loved by him.

You have to understand that apart from God, nothing and nobody can be independent. God's plan is to fashion the human being into two separate people in order to create a healthy situation of dependence, yearning and mutual giving. The human being that God created is not meant to be alone because then they would have no one to give to, no one to grow with and nothing to strive for. The question should be asked; why did God not create identical twins? The answer is that God being the king of kings and the Lord of lords, in order to maximize giving, the recipient must be different from the giver.

God is the creator that knows the end from the beginning. If the two are identical, giving can occur but it is limited. One would give based on his or her needs. To be a sincere giver, the giver must take into account what the receiver needs and not only what the giver wants. This is wisdom you need to understand that by giving to someone with different needs, a person is trained to think and give in terms other than his or her own. As we fully understand that the Bible is the Word of God and a path to spiritual growth. In order to grow and propagate, we need one another; therefore two beings were created. And to maximize growth, the beings need to be different, and so men and women were created by God as different beings.

God created a man and a woman as unique beings and I believe that women were created with an extra dose of wisdom and understanding. Women have the ability to enter something and understand it from the inside which is called "inner reasoning." Men tend to have the understanding that comes from outside. This is the type of understanding that tends to be more connected to facts and figures. The modern society loses a huge asset when only one of these intellectual aspects is valued. As everyone knows that two eyes can give a better and a more accurate view of things than a single eye.

So, seeing things from both the male and the female perspectives makes our understanding of life more complete. Think about this for a moment, the brain of a man and that of a woman is wired in quite different ways. A man and a woman don't think alike, because they have different behavioral patterns as well as having different areas of interest and performance of excellence. May I encourage any man that wants to enjoy his marital life with long life to stop quarrelling with his wife and realize that men and women are not wired the same way?

We should all appreciate that gender is a pivotal quality in each person's identity but understand that men and women are fully equal but different and that difference is very much important. Each gender has its own unique talents and nature that they can give to one another and help each other along the way to a successful marital life. God, in His infinite wisdom, created human beings in two distinct genders in order to enable them to complement and fulfill one another's purpose in life. Husband and wife should always appreciate one another and use their special gift to be a blessing always. Since the genders are different, it would be unnecessary to force or expect both husband and wife to conduct identically. What helps the husband will not necessarily help the wife and vice-versa.

Every husband should realize that his relationship with his wife is just like the relationship of his wife with her mother. Your wife will treat you the way she treats her mother. A woman can play many different roles that include that of a mother, business woman, teacher and wife but all of them as a woman. When a person is asked what she does, she often responds by naming her career only. But the truth is that she is not just a doctor, an engineer, a secretary, a teacher, etc.

You can be one of the women that fulfill their unique potentials this way. You can be this woman! She is clothed with strength and dignity: she can laugh at the days to come. She speaks with wisdom and faithful instructions are on her tongues. She watches over the affairs of her household and does not eat the bread of idleness. Many women do noble things, but you can surpass them all. Charm is deceptive, and beauty is fleeting, but a woman who fears the Lord is to be praised.

Hear what the Bible says that, "The man who finds a wife finds a treasure and receives favour from the Lord. The good wife builds her home with her hands, but the foolish wife tears hers down". (Proverb 18: 22.) This is a two fold blessing. I believe God's favour is upon all who carry out His original creative purpose to multiply and replenish the earth. You have to understand that Satan is trying all he can do on this generation to sabotage the institution of marriage because almost two-thirds of people under 35 years of age believe it is important, and as a fashion or the norm to co-habit before marriage, while a fifth of all single people have no interest in getting married. This is an attempt of Satan to put people off marriage by messing up their mind while they are co-habiting.

It is pathetic that the Children Society should believe that marriage has nothing to do with the reality of family life and that no one should discriminate by saying that parents should be married. I believe that the spirit behind the children society idea about marriage is the spirit of Satan to confuse and to kill the institution of marriage that God ordained. One can say that all that the Children Society has achieved is to encourage men and women to co-habit and have children without getting married, contrary to what God says. God designed marriage that a man and a woman should have companionship in marriage; not a woman and another woman or a man with another man nor a man or woman with an animal.

A wise woman will have the attitude of saying to her husband, "whatever you think". There is a lot of wisdom goodness in this kind of behavior. I believe that your husband will enjoy it once in a while that, you as the wife keep quiet and turn to him adoringly as you say "whatever you think". Furthermore, may I give you this hint as a lovely wife that your husband will appreciate it if you would not always tell him that he took the wrong turn or tell him how to talk to the waiter or what to order or what he should eat every time you are eating out.

The truth is that every husband wants to have the assurance that he has the respect and trust from his wife constantly. Married women should believe this truth that, "What a man keeps hearing every time, he believes it". So, stop telling your husband that he is always making wrong decisions or always making mistakes if you want him to be the best husband that you want him to be.

This is a self-fulfilling belief of women that "If a wife does not want or does not expect her husband to succeed in life, he is most likely may not succeed. May I say that, "nit picking, frequent correction, I know a better way," attitude is destructive on many levels to your husband personality and to your marriage. Men don't enjoy spending time with anyone pulling their male ego to the ground either directly or indirectly. Most of the time, many husbands don't see correction from his wife as something for his good, but rather see it as an attack that is emasculating, depressing and destructive.

The truth is that any wife that is always judgmental and criticizing her husband is not liberated or egalitarian but a quick way for divorce by destroying her own home by herself. A good wife knows that her husband is not a project or a work in progress or a piece of clay for her to mold into what she wants him to be, and as well as the fact that her husband is not a child. I want every good wife to understand that your belief in your husband's abilities and potentials will inspire him to greater height, but Nagging and criticizing will drag him down.

In marriage, husband and wife have to appreciate, respect and love one another, no matter what their situation may look like. Allow your spouse to see the best in you that you cannot see in yourself, and be your best friend in the whole world. You need to understand that you can disagree to agree so that your spouse can still be the greatest person in your life when you don't live in the standard of this world. Every husband normally wants to play the hero to his wife especially when she is fearful or unhappy.

A man may feels like a failure if he cannot be there for his wife and she may not realize how vulnerable her husband is, and how much he needs love too. A woman of purpose must appreciate and welcome her husband when he comes back home even though she may not feel like talking to him. For the Bible says, "Wives, be subject (be submissive and adapt yourself) to your own husbands as (a service) to the Lord." (Ephesians 5:22) This is one of the domestic duty or service of a believer's wife to her husband as a service to God.

It is not a good idea for any wife to bombard her husband as soon as he comes back home with something like this! "Take your child; I can't stand your baby for another minute". Well, on the part of her husband response; he should really understand and hug his wife and say something like this. Well done, I can understand that you are tired; I will try whatever I can do to help looking after the baby with a smile. I can tell you that the attitude of his wife will change immediately. Likewise, on the part of the husband that is at home waiting for his wife to come back. He should not say to his wife's welcome greetings with something like this? "Did you remember to take my suits to the cleaners?

There need to be a balance in the way we use the tone of our voice not to cause offence to the other person. We should always remember that the Bible says that every one of us is the image of God. So we should not mistreat or subject one another as inferior. I believe that your spouse is part of your destiny to take you to greater height if you allow everything to work as God ordained. Then, don't mistreat the work that has already been done by God for your good.

May I encourage every husband and wife reading this book to realize that marriage is not about who has what job or who is bringing the most money home, but the attitude to treat one another as we wants us to be treated to the glory of God. I want every wife to know that if you treat your husband like a king, he will treat you like a queen. For instance, a wife may say to her husband something like this: "Thanks for giving the kids their bath tonight" or "Thanks for picking up dinner, it was a big help" or "Thanks for tidying up the house."

As a godly wife, may I suggest to you to always focus on the task that your husband were able to get done rather than the long list of chores left undone and let him know that you are proud of him. You should say something like: "You handled that situation as a gentle man" or "You were so patient with our son tonight" or "You dealt with that crisis at school so maturely sparing me screaming at the principal". Many men slug it out with their wife for not respecting them enough day after day and it is never a good ending.

Men want to be love and respected so badly that they keep ignoring negative vibes despite the lack of positive reinforcement. Many husbands want peace in their home by acting like servants to their wife, despite not being treated wrongly. Of course, there are many situations where it is the other way round. I can understand that there are many women who have tried everything they can to treat their husbands like a king, but is still not treating them well. I know there are women who are victims of constant abuse by their husband. Please, do not get me wrong.

For any man or woman who mistreats his or her spouse in a domestic violence is wrong. Domestic violence is an abuse of the highest order of marital relationship. Every married woman should appreciate, respect and love her husband and affirm in words too that they love him. Men too need to hear the affirmation of love from their wife constantly as their wife expects to hear it from their husband. Women are so use to focus on their own needs for love from men so much that, it is easy for them to forget the reciprocal responsibilities.

The bible says that "A virtuous and worthy wife (earnest and strong in character) is a crowing joy to her husband, but she who makes him ashamed is as rottenness in his bones." (Proverb 12:4.) This is to say that a morally strong woman both in strength or body is a crown to her husband, but the weakling contracts and communicates such disease as bring rottenness to the bone. What I am saying here to every married woman is to behave appropriately and lovingly to her husband, but this requires lot of efforts and going an extra mile to see that your marriage works stronger every day, than nagging and fighting your husband for every small issue. Every wife must understand that screaming at her husband is not a good attitude that will help any marriage to succeed.

Marriage is about a man and a woman working together and is an institution which can be found in every human culture on the surface of the earth ordained by God. Although the forms and rules differ culturally, but it always involve some form of legal and legitimate sexual relationship. Both the husband and wife need one another according to the marriage that God instituted. You need to know that appreciating your spouse by giving to one another the due respect and showering love, is the basis for a stronger marriage.

Let every man that wants a good marriage affirm this confession!

I am a man of covenant
I will love my wife as Christ love the church.
I will pray with my wife and for our children always.
I will appreciate my wife by being a good listener and a good husband.
All this I will do in the name of the father, the son and the Holy Spirit.
Amen

CHAPTER 5

Divorce is an Abuse

I know that when somebody doesn't understand the importance of a thing, they may likely abuse it. That is the reason why many husband and wife go for divorce because they don't understand the importance of marriage that God designed. Hear what the Bible says, "And did not God make (you and your wife) one (flesh)? Did not one make you and preserve your spirit alive? And why (did God made you two) one? Because He sought a godly offspring (from your union)! Therefore take heed to yourselves, and let no one deal treacherously and be faithless to the wife of his youth. For the Lord, the God of Israel says: I hate divorce and marital separation and him who covers his garment i.e. his wife, with violence. Therefore keep a watch upon your spirit, that it may be controlled by my spirit that you deal not treacherously and faithlessly with your marriage mate." (Malachi 2:15-16.)

The Bible passage here expresses God's hatred of divorce—putting away. May I encourage that anyone with God intelligence does not act that way; for what did that one do, who was seeking offspring from God? So watch out for your feelings lest you be unfaithful to the wife of your youth. God made two persons out of one in the beginning—the man and his wife. But the problem in marriage is that when one of you is unfaithful, he or she cannot have the satisfaction and joy which come by being faithful.

The Bible gives two clear grounds for divorce i.e. (1) (sexual immorality.) Hear this, "But I tell you, whoever dismisses and repudiate and divorce his wife, except on the grounds of unfaithfulness (sexual immorality), causes her to commit adultery, and whoever marries a woman who has been divorced commits adultery." (Matthew 5:32.) (2). (Abandonment by an unbeliever.) For the Bible says "But if the unbelieving partner (actually) leaves, let him do so; in such (cases the remaining) brother or sister is not morally bound. But God has called us to peace." (1 Corinthians 7:15.)

Even in these two instances, though divorce is not required or even encouraged. The most that can be said is that sexual immorality and abandonment are grounds (an allowance) for divorce. Confession, forgiveness, reconciliation, restoration/counseling are always the first steps. The terrible things nowadays is that the divorce rate among the Christian or to say church goers is higher that the secular world.

Let me challenge you today and ask you? What kind of believer are you if you cannot forgive one another. Jesus said, "For if you forgive people their trespasses (there reckless and willful sins, leaving them, letting them go, and giving up resentment), your heavenly Father will also forgive you. But if you do not forgive others their trespasses (their reckless and willful sins, leaving them, letting them go, and giving up resentment), neither will your Father forgive you your trespasses." (Matthew 6:14.) You have to understand what Jesus was saying here and practice it daily because it is one of the conditions of answered prayer.

Many Christian marriages are not good news to write home about nowadays because of the husband and wife behaviour and attitude to one another. The divorce rate is so high in Christian fold nowadays than in the secular world due to lack of truthful teaching and godly teachers on marital relationship. The teaching of godly patient, forgiveness, endurance, tolerance, long-suffering and perseverance in marriage is not being encouraged in most churches these days as it should be.

Why should a pastor advice a church member to divorce her husband? The pastor have his own wife, but still wants to sleep with a church member's wife and mess up somebody else marriage. This is not what the Scriptures teach us that any man or any Pastor should do or advice. The sad thing about Christian divorcing these days is now at an alarming rate that even Pastors who knows the consequences of divorce also divorce his wife and Pastor's wife divorce her husband.

May I encourage you with the Word of God that say, "For you have need of steadfast patience and endurance, so that you may perform and fully accomplish the will of God, and thus receive and carry away (and enjoy to the full) what is promised." (Hebrews 10:36) This is why every Christian is to hold the original confidence steadfast unto the end. You need to forgive one another on a daily basis with steadfast patience and endurance so that you can live in the will of God.

Jesus give explanation to the people, "But He said to them, you are the ones who declare yourselves just and upright before men, but God knows your hearts. For what is exalted and highly thought of among men is detestable and abhorrent (an abomination) in the sight of God. Until John came, there were the Law and the Prophets; since then the good news (the Gospel) of the Kingdom of God is being preached, and everyone strives violently to go in (would force his own way rather than God's way into it). Yet it is easier for heaven and earth to pass away than for one dot of the Law to fail and become void. Whoever divorces (dismisses and repudiates) his wife and marries another commits adultery, and he who marries a woman who is divorced from her husband commits adultery." (Luke16:15-18.)

The Scriptures made it clear for us to understand the issues regarding marital relationship, however many Christian tend to pick and choose the part of the Word of God that suits them. I believe this is not right. Let us try as much as possible to follow what the Bible says. You should understand that the Word of truth is one of the agents that make men new creature. Being a new creature, you should be swift to hear, slow to speak, and slow to wrath. The wrath of man cannot work the righteousness that God requires. That is why the Bible says, "But be doers of the Word (obey the message), and not merely listeners to it, betraying yourselves (into deception by reasoning contrary to the truth)." (James 1:22.)

Let us read the Word of God (Bible) daily and obey because it is the book that reveals the mind of God, the state of man, the way of salvation, the doom of sinners and the happiness of believers. Its doctrine is holy, its precepts binding, its histories are true and it's decisions immutable. The Bible is the book of correction, inspiration and a way of life to every true believing child of God with salvation through Jesus Christ. That is why you have to understand that your salvation is an experience with God, and not with a church, friends, a society or club.

Now let me progress to the area of Christian parenting. Every godly parent must teach their children to give the Word of God the first place in their heart. I believe that anyone who is full of God's Word will manifest the fullness of His presence and the Holy Spirit will dwell in such individual. May I let you know that you can find encouragement and victory in the Word of God daily and believe all the promises in it and not what you may be going through or your situation? Whatever positions you find yourself in life, always believe what the Word of God says about you, your spouse or your children and not what your situation look like.

Hear what the Bible says, "So (as the result of the Messiah's intervention) they shall (reverently) fear the name of the Lord from the west, and His glory from the rising of the sun. When the enemy shall come in like a flood, the Spirit of the Lord will lift up a standard against him and put him to flight (for He will come like a rushing stream which the breath of the Lord drives." (Isaiah 59:19.) May I encourage you that trusting God above your situation and circumstances is essential in your relationship with Him?

This is one of the reasons you have to be filled with the Word of God daily because it is good for your physical and spiritual health and well-being. You have to understand that Satan will not use a bigger annoying thing to fight you but very small thing when you are very weak to defend yourself. He will create a misunderstanding between you and your spouse with those little annoying things and turn it into a big thing to mess up your home. You have to take charge of situation with prayer and fasting before it gets out of hand when you notice that Satan is raising its ugly head in your home.

Men complain that their wife do all sorts of little annoying things such as leaving the top of the toothpaste on the bathroom sink or squeezing the toothpaste in the middle. She is used to watching television very late in the night and this will result in her not waking up in time for work. This has always resort to a blank stare or a quick okay from his wife.

Similarly the wife complains such things that her husband is always putting dirty clothing's on the floor, which is very common among men. This is one of the very little things that can be annoying and should be avoided. When any of these situations arises, the best thing to do is to speak nicely and apologize to your spouse in a loving and gentle manner that will not cause an offence. You have to understand that gentleness will disarm the most furious, but angry words spoken will produce wrath.

For you to have a strong marital relationship, you have to understand that a fool will make his wrath known at once when he is offended, but a wise man will hold his peace. You should know that, "A fool's wrath is quickly and openly known, but a prudent man ignores an insult." (Proverb 12:16.) You need to yield to this profound warning. When you do this, you will have peace at home with your spouse and everyone around you. You need patience everyday to ignore insults from your spouse.

You do not need to be angry with your spouse, as he or she is part of your ministry and your destiny. If you hate your spouse, and move out of your matrimonial home, you start to hate your destiny. From this stage, different things will start to happen and you will start to yield to your flesh.

Then you will start to look for relationship in the wrong places and it may result into something you may regret later in life of the mistake you have created for your children because you did not have enough patience.

Hear what the Bible say, "Drink waters out of your own cistern (of a pure marriage relationship), and fresh running waters out of your own well. Should your offspring be dispersed abroad as water brooks in the streets? (Confine yourself to your own wife) let your children be for you alone, and not the children of strangers with you. Let your fountain (of human life) be blessed (with the reward of fidelity), and rejoice in the wife of your youth. Let her be as the loving hind and pleasant doe (tender, gentle, attractive)—let her bosom satisfy you at all times, and always be transported with delight in her love." (Proverb 5:15-20.)

CHAPTER 6

Believe the Word of God, and Not Your Situation!

Let somebody that accepts the Lord Jesus Christ as His Lord and Saviour; accept as true the authority of the Word of God as a whole. This is to confirm to you that Jesus Christ testify definitely and specifically to the Divine authority of the whole Scriptures. The Jews divided the Old Testament into three parts—the Law, the Prophets, and the Psalms—and Jesus Christ takes up each of these parts and sets the stamp of His authority upon it. He said, "So men are called gods (by the Law), men to whom God's message came—and the Scripture cannot be set aside or cancelled or broken or annulled." (John 10:35.)

Therefore teaching the absolute accuracy and inviolability of the Word of God is necessary and to believe and obey is paramount. I want you to understand what Jesus Christ is saying here that, "For truly I tell you, until the sky and earth pass away and perish, not one smallest letter nor one little hook (identifying certain Hebrew letters) will pass from the Law until all things (it foreshadows) are accomplished." (Matt. 5:18.) Jesus Christ declares the Scripture as the absolutely truth, down to the smallest letter or point of a letter. So if we accept the authority of Christ we must accept the Divine authority of the entire Bible.

You need to understand, believe, and obey what the Scriptures is concerning your marriage, and not what your situation look like. As a believer of the Lord Jesus Christ, you have a new teacher and reminder of truth, the Holy Spirit, for Jesus said, "But the comforter (Counselor,

Helper, Intercessor, Advocate, Strengthener, Standby), the Holy Spirit, Whom the Father will send in my name (in my place, to represent me and act on my behalf), He will teach you all things. And He will cause you to recall (will remind you of, bring to your remembrance) everything I have told you." (John 14:26.)

At this point we see that not only was the teaching of the Apostles to be fully inspired, but also their recollection of what Christ Himself taught. We are sometimes asked how we know that the Apostles correctly reported what Jesus said—"may they not have forgotten?" True, they might forget, but Christ Himself tells us that in the Gospels we have not the Apostles' recollection of what He said but the Holy Ghost's recollection and the Spirit of God never forget.

Jesus said to his Apostles, "**I still have many things to say to you, but you cannot bear *them* now. However, when He, the Spirit of truth, has come, He will guide you into all truth; for He will not speak on His own *authority,* but whatever He hears He will speak; and He will tell you things to come. He will glorify me, for He will take of what is mine and declare *it* to you.**" (John 16:12-14.) Christ said that the Holy Ghost will guide the Apostles into "all truth" therefore in the Bible teaching; we have the whole sphere of God's truth.

As you already may be aware that this is an old argument, but a very satisfactory one! For the Bible consists of sixty-six books, written by more than thirty different men, extending in the period of its composition over more than fifteen hundred years; written in three different languages, in many different countries, and by men on every plane of social life—from the herdsman and fisherman and cheap politician up to the king upon his throne; written under all sorts of circumstances; yet in all this wonderful conglomeration we find an absolute unity of thought. A wonderful thing about it is that this unity does not appear on the surface. On the surface there is oftentimes apparent contradiction, and the unity only comes out after deep and protracted study.

More wonderful yet is the organic character of this unity, beginning in the first book and growing till you come to its culmination in the last book of the Bible. We have first the seed, then the plant, then the bud, then the blossom, then the ripened fruit. So in this marvelous temple of God's truth which we call the Bible, whose stones have been quarried at periods of time and in places so remote from one another, but where every smallest part fits each other part, we are forced to say that back of the human hands that wrought was the Master-mind that thought.

It is quite fashionable in some quarters to compare the teachings of the Bible with the teachings of Zoroaster, and Buddha, and Confucius, and Epictetus, and Socrates, and Marcus Aurelius Antonius, and a number of other heathen authors. The difference between the teachings of the Bible and those of these men is found in three points. The first point is that the Bible has in it nothing but truth, while all the others have truth mixed with error. It is true Socrates taught how a philosopher ought to die; he also taught how a woman of the town ought to conduct her business. There are Jewels in the teachings of these men, but (as Joseph Cook once said) they are "jewels picked out of the mud."

The second point you have to understand without the shadow of a doubt is that the Bible contains *all* truth. There is not a truth to be found anywhere on moral or spiritual subjects that you cannot find in substance within the covers of that old Book. I have often, when speaking upon this subject, asked anyone to bring me a single truth on moral or spiritual subjects, who, upon reflection, I could not find within the covers of this Book, and no one has ever been able to do so. I have taken pains to compare some of the better teachings of the secular world, with those of the Bible. They indeed have jewels of thought, but they are, whether they knew it or not, stolen jewels, and stolen from the very Book they ridicule.

The third point is the superiority of the Bible which contains more truth than all other books together. Get together from all literature of ancient and modern times all the beautiful thoughts you can; put away all the rubbish; put all these truths that you have culled from the literature of all ages into one book, and as the result, even then you will not have a book that will take the place of this one Book. This is not a large Book. I hold in my hand a copy that I carry in my vest pocket and yet in this one little Book there is more of truth than in all the books which man has produced in all the ages of his history. How will you account for it? There is only one rational way. This is not man's Book, but God's Book.

This book has always been hated. No sooner was it given to the world than it met the hatred of men, and they tried to stamp it out. Celsius tried it by the brilliancy of his genius, Porphyry by the depth of his philosophy; but they failed, Lucian directed against it the shafts of his ridicule, Diocletian the power of the Roman Empire; but they failed. Edicts, backed by all the power of the Empire, were issued that every Bible should be burned, and that everyone who had a Bible should be put to death. You have to understand that two things speak for the divinity of the Bible—the character of those who accept it, and, equally, the character of those who reject it. I do not mean by this that every man who professes to believe the Bible is better than every man that does not, but show me a man living an unselfish, devoted life, one who without reservation has surrendered himself to do the will of God, and I will show you a man who believes the Bible to be God's Word. On the other hand, show me a man who rejects the Divine authority of that Book, and I will show you a man living a life of greed, or lust, or spiritual pride, or self-will.

Suppose you have a book purporting to be by a certain author, and the people best acquainted with that author say it is his, and the people least acquainted with him say it is not; which will you believe? Now, the people best acquainted with God say the Bible is His Book; those who are least acquainted with God say it is not. Which will you believe?

Moreover, as men grow better they are more likely to accept the Bible, and as they grow worse they are more likely to reject it. We have all known men who were both sinful and unbelieving who, by forsaking their sin, lost their unbelief. Did any of us ever know a man who was sinful and believing who, by forsaking his sin, lost his faith? The nearer men live to God, the more confident they are that the Bible is God's Word; the farther they get away from Him, the more confident they are that it is not.

Where is the stronghold of the Bible? In the unselfish and happy homes! Where is the stronghold of infidelity? The gambling hell, the drinking saloon and the brothel! If a man should walk into a saloon and lay a Bible down upon the bar, and order a drink, we should think there was a strange incongruity in his actions, but if he should lay any infidel writing upon the bar and order a drink, we would not feel that there was any incongruity.

I can tell you emphatically that there is more power in that little Book to save men and purify, gladden and beautify their lives, than in all other literature put together—more power to lift men up to God. A stream never rises higher than its source, and a Book that has a power to lift men up to God that no other book has, must have come down from God in a way that no other book was.

There is no other book has the power to elevate not only individuals but husbands and wives, communities and nations that this Book has? A brilliant Unitarian writer, in trying to disprove the inspiration of the Bible says: "How irreligious to charge an infinite God with having written His whole Word in so small a book." He does not see how his argument can be turned against himself. What a testimony it is to the divinity of this Book that such infinite wisdom is stored away in so small a compass.

Every thoughtful person that starts to study the Bible finds many things with which he does not agree, but as he goes on studying and growing in likeness to God, the nearer he gets to God the nearer he gets to the Bible. The nearer and nearer we get to God's standpoint, the less and less becomes the disagreement between us and the Bible. What is the inevitable mathematical conclusion? When we get where God is, we and the Bible will meet. In other words, the Bible was written from God's standpoint.

May I encourage you as a reader of this book to understand that we began with God and shall end with God? We began with the testimony of the second person of the Trinity, and shall close with that of the third person of the Trinity. The Holy Spirit sets His seal in the soul of every believer to the Divine authority of the Bible. It is possible to get to a place where we need no argument to prove that the Bible is God's Word. Christ says, "My sheep know my voice," and God's children know His voice, and I know that the voice that speaks to me from the pages of that Book is the voice of my Father. You will sometimes meet a pious old lady, who tells you that she knows that the Bible is God's Word, and when you ask her for a reason for believing that it is God's Word she can give you none, She simply says, "I know it is God's Word."

You may say, Charles; "That is mere superstition." Not at all! She is one of Christ's sheep, and recognizes her Shepherd's voice from every other voice. She is one of God's children, and knows the voice which speaks to her from the Bible is the voice of God. She is above argument. Everyone can have that testimony as Jesus said, "If any man desires to do His will (God's pleasure), he will know (have the needed illumination to recognize, and can tell for himself) whether the teaching is from God or whether I am speaking from myself and of my own accord and on my own authority." (John 7:17.)

For you to have this experience, just surrender your will to the will of God, no matter where it carries you, and you will put yourself in such an attitude toward God that when you read this Book you will recognize that the voice that speaks to you from the Bible is the voice of the God to whom you have surrendered your will.

Every husband and wife must believe the Word of God for whatever challenges they may be going through. Begin to confess and believe what the Bible says concerning the situation that may be of challenge to you. Get your eyes off your situation and focus on God. Subsequently learn to speak positively to yourself and situation daily no matter what the situation look like. By the word of faith in your mouth, your actions will follow suit. Let everyone that believes that Jesus Christ is the son of God changes the words of their mouth to positive confession and change their ways. You have to learn and prophesy the Word of God to yourself, your spouse, your children, your marriage and your finances frequently.

You have to understand the truth that the words you speaks are like seeds. By speaking positive or negative words aloud, you are speaking them into existence and planting them into your sub-conscious mind and they will take on a life of their own. These words will take root, grow and produce fruit of a positive or negative kind. Let each person get up in the morning, look in the mirror and confess to him or herself and say, "I am valuable, loved, and blessed": My marriage is blessed; my spouse and children are blessed: I am a store house of God blessing: God has a great plan for my life: I have favor wherever I go: God's favors will chase me and overtake me: Everything I touch will prosper and succeed: I am excited about my future: I am rising to a new level of well-being, success and victory in my life and marriage, in Jesus name. Amen.

For instance, your children too need to hear the positive affirmation frequently. Words such as "I love you; I believe in you; I think you are great". Your children want your attention, recognition, acceptance, approval, and respect. If your child knows he or she has these, they are more likely to take your guidance. But you can't just assume that they know how you feel about them. You have to tell your children, not only in words, but also in your actions and your general attitude. When you encourage your children, you are nourishing their self-worth and raising their self-esteem which will in turn help them to grow into a confident adult sure of themselves and their ability to achieve the things they set out to do.

The art of positive communication with your teenagers is a legacy you can pass on. The way you communicate with your children will dictate the way they communicate with others. May I encourage you to begin and speak positive confession into your life especially your marital relationship frequently. You need to understand that there are some blessings that it will not manifest until it is spoken out positively. This is why you have to make positive pronouncement on yourself, your children and marriage always. Speak words like "My marriage is strong and successful." God wants you to be successful in your marital relationship.

As Christians, husband and wife need to understand what Apostle Paul is saying that whatever you do to one another, you are doing it as a service to the Lord. "Be subject to one another out of reverence for Christ (the Messiah, the Anointed One). Wives, be subject (be submissive and adapt yourselves) to your own husbands as (a service) to the Lord. For the husband is the head of the wife as Christ is the Head of the church, Himself the saviour of (His) body. As the church is subject to Christ, so let wives also be subject in everything to their husbands. Husbands, love your wives, as Christ loved the church and gave Himself up for her." (Ephesians 5:21-23.)

You need to understand that in everyone's life, there will be a time to encounter circumstances that can cause you to grow negative, bitter or disappointed in yourself or in God. But I want you to remember what Apostle Paul said, "I do not consider, brethren, that I have captured and made it my own (yet); but one thing I do (it is my own aspiration); forgetting what lies behind and straining forward to what lies ahead; I press on towards the goal to win the (supreme and heavenly) prize to which God in Christ Jesus is calling us upward." (Philippians 3:13-14.) You see over here, Apostle Paul is saying to us that we should not be dwelling on yesterday's disappointments or our past failures.

We should not be thinking about what we should have done or not done. Let us leave all that behind us and press ahead for the good things God has in store for us. Friend, I know it appears difficult but you must be determined and refuse to be trapped in your past. Do not let your past destroy your future; Start pressing on, continue straining forward, believing that God has great things in store for you. You need to follow after and press toward the prize others have already gained in marital success to the glory of God.

Let the victory spirit begin to rise within you like David in the Bible. Before he became king of Israel, he went out patrolling one day with his men, but while he was away, some bandits attacked his city. Their homes were burnt, their possession stolen; their women and children were kidnapped. When David and his men came back, they were devastated. They cried until they could cry no more. Then David made a decision that changed their destiny. The Bible says, "David encouraged and strengthened himself in the Lord." (1 Samuel 30:6.) He and his men got up and went after their enemy. They attacked the enemy and recovered everything. David and his men persevered and God supernaturally helped them to recover everything that had been stolen.

Let me encourage you to get out of defeat mentality and start thinking and believing positively from today? It is not over until it is over. Say to yourself that you are not going to give up and you will not settle for mediocrity. Start to believe every Word of God and start to believe for the best. Remember that the Bible did not present David as a perfect man. He made mistakes like you and I, but he confessed his faults and pray, God renew a right, persevering and steadfast spirit within him.

Similarly, you too can pray and say: "Father, help me to get rid of negative thoughts and attitude. Help me to get rid of self-pity and not to give up easily in my marriage and all other area of my life because quitter never wins and winners never quit. Lord, renew your right spirit within me in Jesus name." Amen. As I have said in the earlier chapter that when you have done everything you know how to do, just hold on to God patiently and prayerfully.

The Bible say that the vision is for an appointed time, for it will come to pass. Start to believe that whatever the enemy meant for evil will be turned around and used by God to your advantage. From today, develop a delivery and sustaining faith in every area of your life especially your marriage. Delivery faith is when God instantly turns your situation around. It is great when this happens but you must realize that it takes a deeper walk with God to have a sustaining faith. This is when circumstances do not change immediately. Be steadfast, patient and say "God, no matter what I am going through, I will not be moved; this situation is not going to defeat me in Jesus name. Amen.

Whatever may be your marital challenge that you are facing right now, I pray and trust God for you that it will be what He will use to promote you for His glory. God has promised that He will turn your challenges into stepping stones for advancement. God wants to do new and unusual things in your life if you surrender all to Him. He is looking for people who will trust Him with their whole heart and not limit Him with their small-mentality.

God is simply looking for a willing heart and not ability, but for availability, by obedience and giving Him the little you have. He will take it and multiply it with increase. I believe that one day, you will look back at what you consider as a setback, and you will realize that God used that thing of adversity to refine you, mold you, shape you and prepare you for good things to come.

You need to understand that adversity often pushes people that trust God into their divine destiny. You will be amazed at what you can accomplish when God puts a little pressure on you and you get out of that comfort zone and step over into the faith zone. God will allow pressure to push and stretch you to the limit so that you will be able to be humble and disciplined for your next assignment. God knows His gifts, ability and talents He placed in you: He will do everything necessary to get them into manifestation, when you surrender completely to Him.

I want you to understand that everyone has an area in his or her life where constantly struggles occur even putting in all efforts to change a bad habit or an addiction. You need to ask God for His grace to overcome such situation be it in your marriage or otherwise because there is some bad situation or habit that only God can help us to overcome. Ask God to reveal what is keeping you bound and what to do to break the bondage of such bad situation or habit.

Ask God to reveal to you if you have deep roots for bitterness, unforgiving spirit or anger that need to be dug out and eradicate completely. Finally, when God reveals it to you, be quick to deal with it and be willing to make a change. Do not allow the poison of the past to contaminate your future.

David said, "Search me (thoroughly), O God, and know my heart! Try me and know my thoughts! And see if there is any wicked or hurtful way in me, and lead me in the way everlasting." (Psalms 139:23-24.) You have to search your heart and ask God to uproot any root of negative power and thoughts that may be the problem in your marital life.

I pray that your struggle will be an opportunity for advancement and promotion in Jesus name. That very thing i.e. old habit of negative situation in your marriage that you are fighting against so badly will be the springboard that will catapult you to a new level of joy and peace in Jesus name. May I encourage you that if you want to experience the goodness of God in your marriage and in every area of your life from today, your heart must be opened for obedience so that you may receive from Him? You need to have time to make a difference in your marriage and encourage others especially your spouse, to help them feel better about their life.

As a child of God, keep your heart of compassion open so that you can be on the look-out for people you can be a blessing to everyday. Jesus Christ is a good example: He has time to bless and help other people: He was never too busy with his own plan. Many people are self-centered and selfish nowadays and are not experiencing life to the full because they have closed their heart of compassion. What I want you to know is that if you focus on meeting other people's needs, God will always make sure your needs are met when you trust Him completely.

I know that many people may be smiling on the outside but are badly hurt inside. Only God can see a person's heart and knows when that person is hurting or lonely. My friend, never ignore the feeling of compassion inside you, learn to be sensitive to God's divine love. I pray that God will direct your steps and guide you if you let him. Many times, it may appear unwise, foolish or over-spiritual when you try to show compassion but it is better to give a word of encouragement than to let another man or woman lose his or her life. You never know, you may be the last hope for someone's survival. God may be telling you about a person's problems and how you can reach out to help. For example, if someone's name keeps coming up in your mind and you have a feeling of compassion for the person, pray for the person and call on the person if you have the means. Let the person knows that God love him or her and that you care too.

Satan has deceived many women in recent times by robbing them of their marriage, joy, peace of mind and their children. The Women League group claimed that women do not need men at home anymore. This is the lie Satan is telling certain groups of women who prefer to disobey God and yield to self-deceit. Many homes have been destroyed as a result of the fact that some schools of thought believe that a woman can successfully raise children without the assistance of a man.

I believe that this has resulted to negative effects on children and many of them are turning to drugs, alcoholics, prostitution, crime, vandalism, etc, because of the lack of a male role model at home. Look at what happened next, Satan created a mishmash of saber-waving to wipe the creamed potato from the eyebrow of some women and gave them a life according to their wish. With this entire happening, marital boundaries and responsibilities have become blurred.

May I encourage you today so that you can understand that love is the greatest weapon of the power of the Holy Spirit that can resist anti-marriage forces? When a married couple has a misunderstanding, the test for the type of love in question is not who should apologize first, nor who is right or wrong. The person that says, it is the partner who is wrong that should apologize, fails the test of love. The truth of a strong marriage is the husband or the wife that is right but apologizes to the partner is the person who has the model love of God.

God is Love, but how do we define it? The American Heritage Dictionary defines love as "an intense affection for another person based on familial or personal ties". Often this "intense affection" stems from a sexual attraction for that other person. We love other people, or we say we love other people, when we are attracted to them and when they make us feel good. Notice that a key phrase in the dictionary definition of love is the phrase "based on". This phrase implies that we love conditionally; in other words, we love someone because they

fulfill a condition that we require before we can love them. How many times have you heard or said, "I love you to your spouse," or "I love you because you take good care of me;" or "I love you because you are fun to be with"?

Our love is not only conditional, it is also mercurial. We love based on feelings and emotions that can change from one moment to the next. The divorce rate is extremely high in today's society because husbands and wives supposedly stop loving one another or they "fall out of love". They may go through a rough patch in their marriage, and they no longer "feel" love for their spouse, so they call it quits. The reason for this is that many people did not consult the originator of marriage and they did not follow His guidelines, (The Bible.)

Obviously, the truth is that many people in today's marriages don't understand their marriage vow of "till death do us part" means they can part at the death of their love for their spouse rather than at their physical death as the Scriptures says we should all do. Can I challenge you today if you can really comprehend "unconditional" love? It seems the love that parents have for their children is as close to unconditional love as we can get without the help of God's love in our lives.

I believe every parent understand what I'm saying here that we continue to love our children through good times and bad, and we don't stop loving them if they don't meet the expectations we may have for them. We make a choice to love our children even when we consider them unlovable; our love doesn't stop when we don't "feel" love for them. This is similar to God's love for us, but as we shall see, God's love transcends the human definition of love to a point that is hard for us to comprehend.

The Bible says that, "Dear friends, let us continue to love one another, for love comes from God. Anyone who loves is born of God and knows God. But anyone who does not love does not know God—for God is Love" (1 John 4: 7-8.) This is to prove that we are of God and knowing Him because He is God and we should imitate Him as His children. But how can we even begin to understand this truth? You have to start to understand that, *"For God so loved the world that he gave his only begotten Son, that whosoever believeth in him should not perish, but have everlasting life."* (John 3:16.) So one way God defines His love is in the act of giving.

However, what God gave (or should I say, "who" God gave) was not a mere gift-wrapped present; God sacrificed His only Son so that we, who put our faith in His Son, will not spend eternity separated from Him. This is an amazing love, because we are the ones who choose to reject God, yet it's God who mends the separation through His intense personal sacrifice, and all we have to do is accept His gift.

I want every husband and wife to fully understand the scriptures concerning God's love towards us and we should imitate Him. *"But God commanded his love toward us, in that, while we were yet sinners, Christ died for us."*(Romans 5:8.) May I submit to you that from these verses of the Bible that no conditions placed on God's love for us? Why are we then placing conditions on our spouse? God doesn't say, "as soon as you clean up your act, I'll love you" or does He say, "I'll sacrifice my Son if you promise to love me."

In fact in (Romans 5:8), we find just the opposite. God wants us to know that His love is unconditional, so He sent His Son, Jesus Christ, to die for us while we were still unlovable sinners. We didn't have to get clean, and we didn't have to make any promises to God before we could experience His love. His love for us has always existed, and because of that, He did all the giving and sacrificing long before we were even aware that we needed His love. God is Love and its Unconditional.

The truth is that hatred is the opposite of love. You have to understand that hatred seeks an occasion to provoke enmity and delights in brawls, but love is conciliatory and removes all occasion for trouble. For the Bible says, "Hatred stirs up contentions, but love covers all transgressions." (Proverbs 10:12.) Every husband and wife that wants to have a strong marital relationship should pray for Divine love of God. There are ingredients of Divine love which you need to put into practice daily to achieve peace and joy in your marriage, so that it can be a miracle of completion.

(A). Patience—love passive: no hurry; suffers long; bears, believes, hopes, and endures all things.
(B). Kindness—love in action: never acts rashly or insolently; not inconsistent, puffed up, or proud.
(C). Generosity—love in competition: not envious or jealous.
(D). Humility—love in hiding: no parade; no airs; works then retires
(E). Courtesy—love in society: does not behave unseemly; always polite; at home with all classes; never rude or discourteous!

Unselfishness—love in essence: never selfish, sour, or bitter; seeks only well of others; does not retaliate or seek revenge.

(F). Good temper—love in disposition: never irritated; never resentful.

(G). Righteousness—love in conduct: hates sin; never glad when others go wrong; always gladdened by goodness to others; always slow to expose; always eager to believe the best; always hopeful, always enduring.

(H). Sincerity—love in profession: never boastful and conceited; not a hypocrite; always honest; leaves no impression but what is strictly true; never self-assertive; does not blaze out in passionate anger, nor brood over wrongs; always just, joyful, and truthful; always present.

The bottom line of it all is that the Bible says, "Love never fails (never fades out or becomes obsolete or comes to an end). As for prophesy (the gift of interpreting the divine will and purpose), it will be fulfilled and pass away; as for tongues, they will be destroyed and cease; as for knowledge, it will pass away (it will lose its value and be superseded by truth)." (1 Corinthians 13:8.)

CHAPTER 7

You are What You Watch

You are what you watch nowadays and it is no longer a lazy way to redirect a boring conversation. Questions about viewing preferences have become fraught; the topic is as intimate, revealing and potentially off-putting as discussing how much money you make. It's a rich television age and a demanding one. The selection is now so plentiful and fragmented and good. And deciding among hundreds of channels, on-demand options, DVR, Internet streaming and iPhones requires so much research, planning and commitment that viewers have become proprietary about their choices. Alliances are formed, and so are antipathies. Snobbery takes root. Preferences turn totemic.

The mass audience splintered long ago; now viewers are divided into tribes with their own rituals and rites of passage that make many families to exist on a mental diet of television, motion pictures and slick publications designed to stimulate us. I consider all these to be "junk food". It leads to mental malnutrition and poor emotional and spiritual health that many couples emulate what they watch on the television in their homes. If adults have much difficulty distinguishing fantasy from reality, then the effect the television has on children is serious case for concern. Values are also beamed into children via the television screen and many are negative or at the very least, out of touch with reality.

I believe that your favorite show is a tip-off to your personality, taste and sophistication the way music was before it became virtually free and consumed as much by individual song as artist. The truth of the whole matter is that many things on the television nowadays is a waste of time that even dramas have become more complicated; many of it are serialized and require time and sequential viewing. That is why it is important for you to know and understand that you are your most important critic. Whatever you do, watch or waste your time on, is what you are.

May I say that there is no opinion so vitally important to the well-being of you or your marital life than the opinion you have of yourself. Additionally, you need to know that the most important meetings, briefing and conversation you will ever have are those you have with yourself. Let me encourage you to practice this habit until it is part of your life; to whisper to one another with a kiss every night and say, "I love you and good night". Likewise every parent should have the habit to say to their children every night before bed time "Good night, love you and God bless." By this good habit daily, you will eliminate whatever negative things you may have gone through during the day time.

It is a good idea to protect your mind and that of our spouse in what you watch, read and engage in. Filth going in our mind will eventually come out creating painful lingering consequences. A wife doesn't want to wander if her husband is comparing her to the partially or completely naked woman he saw on the big screen last night and likewise the husband to the wife. You see by allowing these insecurities in your mind against your spouse is not pleasing God because it will bring envy, jealousy and hatred to your relationship, so be careful of what you put into your eye gate that goes into your mind. You might think it doesn't affect you but it does.

No one is immune to sin and that is why you have to look out so that you do not fall under the trick of Satan by what you watch. Believe it now that you are a child of promise and God has already ordained you before the beginning of time so that you do not allow Satan to mess up the life of your offspring and that of your family through your weakness. May I encourage you today to stand firm in the Word of God for your marriage because God did not say that things would be rosy all the time. Actually, the Bible says that Christians are in warfare. We are not fighting against flesh and blood, but against principalities and powers of darkness in high places. Christians should expect to pass through tough times and be prepared and equipped to be winners.

As a child of God, you have to understand that every good thing you have including your marriage and family is the target for Satan as he will like to destroy them but you must not be discouraged as God is with you and in you and is more than all that are against you. Let the faith of God arise in you and start to believe that, "No weapon that is formed against you shall prosper, and every tongue that accuses you in judgment you will condemn. This is the heritage of the servants of the Lord. And their vindication is from me, declares the Lord." (Isaiah 54:17.) This is God's promise for you. He will never fail you nor forsake you, just put your trust in Him because His faithfulness is forever. Yet amid all these things we are more than conquerors and gain a surpassing victory through Him who loved us.

I want you to understand that every successful marriage is not one in which two ideally matched people find each other and live happily ever after from day one. No matter how carefully one selects a partner, married life is not a perfect thing. If people realized this from the beginning, there would be far less trouble within marriage. The God loving couple has their failings, but two such people work on through the years to build a strong relationship that is aligned with the Biblical ideal. To create that ideal marriage is the work of a life time and that is why this book is written just for you so that you may have Marriage a miracle of completion.

CHAPTER 8

Choice of a Spouse

"A pretty face is an attraction, but oh, how vain to be governed in such a serious undertaking by such a trifle. Earthly goods and social position have their value, yet how base and degrading to suffer them to control such a solemn undertaking. Oh yes, watchfulness and prayerfulness is needed in the regulation of our affections." May I encourage everyone to understand that marriage is not to be taken in hand unadvisedly, wantonly or lightly, but reverently, discreetly, advisedly, soberly and in the fear of God? This is to say that every Christian needs to approach the whole matter of marriage in a reverent and honorable manner, always in the fear of God.

I believe in the divine will of God that you may alter your condition of being single if you have not, but must wait on God for direction and heartily entreat Him that if this motion be not of Him, it may not happen. You can be like the manner of Isaac's marrying with Rebecca, and think no marriage can succeed well unless both parties concerned are like-minded. However, you can call the God to witness that which is your desire `to take a wife or a husband, not for lust, but uprightness.

Let me encourage you as you read this book that the passionate expressions which carnal courtiers use, I think, ought to be avoided by those that would marry in the Lord . . . If you think marriage will be in any way prejudicial to your better part, be so kind as to stop reading this book. But if marriage is for you, there should be much prayer over the choice of a future marriage partner.

This is for every younger women to learn from older women to understand and practice daily according to what the Bible says, "These older women must train the younger women to love their husbands and their husbands and their children, to live wisely and be pure, to take care of their homes, to do good, and to be submissive to their husbands. Then they will not bring shame on the word of God." (Titus 2:4-5.) Since husband and wife are to love one another within marriage, it is evident that there must be a caring and loving relationship already in existence before entering upon the marital relationship.

What then is love? And how is it to be recognized? I believe there are three kinds of Love and in the Greek language there are three words which are translated into the one English word 'love'. Eros is one such word, although not found in the New Testament. From this Greek word we translate the English word 'erotic'. Erotic love is that which belongs to the flesh, born of selfish desire, seeking only self—gratification; it is little more than an animal magnetism. It stems from fleshly desires of man's base appetite and it is this erotic love which the world sings about in the sex soaked lyrics of this pop age.

This is the love which the world glories in i.e. (carnal and sensual), and for many marriages this is all that there is from the very beginning of their relationship. Of course, there is a sense in which this natural physical attraction will be present. God has so created man that this physical element will be there. This point is important because Christians have been guilty of seeking to discount physical attraction altogether. Of course we must not lay as much emphasis as the world does.

Although beauty is vain according to (Proverbs 31) nevertheless there ought to be some attraction that draws a couple together. Of course this natural and physical element will come under the sanctifying power of the indwelling Holy Spirit. As Christians, surely it is right that we feel more attracted to one person than we do to another? The highest form of this kind of Love is agape. Agape love is an unconditional love. It loves when all other kind of love quit, and cares when there is no apparent reason to care. This love comes from God into a person when they ask Jesus to come into their heart and to be their Lord and savior.

Phileo is the second Greek word for love. It represents tender affection and fondness. The Bible says, "When they had eaten, Jesus said to Simon Peter, Simon, son of John, do you love me more than these (others do—with reasoning, intentional, spiritual devotion, as one loves the Father)? He said to Him, Yes, Lord, You know that I love you (that I have deep, instinctive, personal affection for you, as for a close friend). He said to him, Feed My lambs," (John 21:15.) "He said to Him, `Yes, Lord; you know that I love you." In his reply, Peter is using the verb phileo. It means affection or fondness. In (John 21:16), Jesus uses agapao and Peter again replies with the phileo verb. Jesus is using one Greek verb for love, but Peter will not use it himself because it expresses the highest form of love that exists.

The highest love that Peter will allow himself to express is this phileo love, a fondness and affection for Christ. The Lord asks him the same question a third time in (John 21:17), and then says to him, "Feed my sheep." When Jesus repeats this question for the last time saying, "Do you love me?" He uses the verb phileo. He descends to Peter's level. This is why Peter was grieved; it appeared to him that the Lord doubted that Peter even had this phileo love for him, and so he replies in verse 17, "Lord, You know all things; You know that I love [phileo—am fond of] You." Peter is humbled.

This verb phileo is usually translated in the New Testament as fondness or having affection for; the type of affection a brother has for a brother. Over and above the Eros physical element, there will be a longing for each other and for each other's company. There will be an emotional satisfaction derived merely from being in each other's company. If Eros speaks of that physical and natural affinity, then phileo speaks of that emotional affinity and oneness.

Agapao is the third verb for love and is used almost exclusively throughout the New Testament to express God's love towards His Son, the world and the Church. The Bible says, "For God so greatly loved and dearly prized the world that He (even) gave up His only begotten (unique) Son, so that whoever believes in (trusts in, clings to, relies on,) Him shall not perish (come to destruction, be lost) but have eternal (everlasting)" (John 3:16): this is the agapao verb. This is the highest form of love that there is.

Hear what the Bible says, "But God demonstrates His own love toward us, in that while we were still sinners, Christ died for us." (Romans 5:8) This again is God's love, agapao, which He commends towards us; this unsearchable, amazing and astounding love of God. This is the very nature of God, and agapao is a love which has its source in God. God is agapao. It is deep seated, purposeful, intelligent, a love in which God's entire personality plays a part. This is the type of love that the husband must have for his wife which is spoken of in (Ephesians 5).

The husband is to love his wife in spite of all her defects and failings. This is a vital message for this generation when the divorce rate is so high even in the church. Secondly, Christ "gave himself for it." Such is His love for the Church that He laid down his life as a sacrifice for her. This agapao love is a sacrificial love which a husband should have for his wife. The highest love that the world can know is this Eros and phileo love. There can be natural and physical attraction for each other and emotional affinity, but the world can go no higher than that. Only the Christian can rise to this agapao level because it is a love which is based upon and flows out of Christ's love for the Church.

When the world so glibly sings and talks about falling in love, it is usually referring to erotic and sensual attraction. On occasions it may go beyond that and encompass emotional attraction, but Christian couples need to have far more than this. They need the love which sanctifies the first two elements. This will stem from their union in Christ; that sacrificial tender, compassionate, caring love which is prepared to give and to love and ask nothing in return. Being in love for a Christian is therefore far more than being attracted by a pretty face or handsome appearance.

I want you to understand the difference between infatuation and true love? Romantic infatuation is almost exclusively based on physical attraction. The person who is infatuated is deprived of judgment and reason. In fact the word infatuation means "To turn to folly and inspire with foolish passion." Romantic infatuation is something that most people experience at some point, and therefore they have the problem of knowing the difference between love and infatuation.

Infatuation and love are different in four main points. Firstly, romantic infatuation may happen suddenly and without warning, whereas love grows and produces a growing relationship between the couple. Secondly romantic infatuation arises from a few characteristics of the other person. The one infatuated knows only a few characteristics of that person and on the basis of those characteristics, which are often connected with physical appearance, they are infatuated. On the other hand, love makes an appraisal of the total personality of the other person. Feelings of love develop in a maturing relationship with the other person which appraises the whole personality, not merely a few characteristics.

Thirdly, an infatuated person sustains a mental picture of the object of infatuation, a mental image based largely on idealization. A few characteristics of the person are dwelt upon and a tremendous fantasy picture of the person's whole character is built upon it. The fantasy image will vanish when they learn about the other's faults, weaknesses and sinfulness; whereas one who truly loves another will constantly check their ideas of that person against the growing awareness of their whole character.

Fourthly, an infatuated person tends to have a false sense of security about the romance. It is based upon wishful thinking and there is a compulsive need for reassurance in the relationship, whereas a person who knows true love tends to have a true sense of security in their relationship, based upon a growing trust, affection and mutual concern. I would therefore advise all young people who feel that they may love someone to give their relationship the test of time and preferably the test of separation. True love between a man and a woman will stand the test of time and separation, whereas infatuation will not stand up to this test. Much watchfulness and prayer are necessary to avoid divorce in later years of marriage.

Let me encourage you if you are a single Christian man or woman of how to find a marriage partner. I have already established that a Christian is only to marry another Christian. For the Bible says that, "He who finds a (true) wife, finds a good thing and obtains favor from the Lord." (Proverbs 18:22.) Further more hear what the scripture says that "A virtuous and worthy wife (earnest and strong in character) is a crowing joy to her husband, but she who makes him ashamed is as rottenness in his bones." (Proverbs 12:4.) A morally strong woman is a crown to her husband, but the weakling contracts and communicates such diseases as bring rottenness to his bones.

Hear this, "House and riches are the inheritance from fathers, but a wise, understanding, and prudent wife is from the Lord." (Proverbs 19:14.) These are two of the great blessing of man. Godly partner must be sought from the Lord, and in finding a suitable marriage partner there must be prayer and seeking. The reason why many Christians find it difficulty in this area is that they do not pray right and do not seek in the right place. Let me encourage you if you are not married yet but still seeking for a Godly spouse to understand that a good wife is from the Lord, for she is the best gift of His providence.

This is for the single only that there is need for prayer and seeking. I believe in all probability the person whom you may marry is now living somewhere on the earth definitely! Start to pray for that person wherever he or she may be. You may say, "but I don't know his name or her name" the Lord does. Do not wait until it is too late. Start to pray now as you will pray when you will meet the person. Pray for sanctification and to walk in holiness. Pray that the Lord in His own time will so arrange His providential dealings that the two of you shall be brought together.

When you do meet with the right person who is your suitable marriage partner, then follow what the Holly Spirit will reveal to you, and not what you may think is right. Today this person may not be the one you think that you want but be careful not to miss your best opportunity. Let me encourage you today that much watchfulness and prayer is needed in the regulation of your affections. Pray now for the one whom you are to marry, if indeed you do marry. Pray that your affections may always be regulated by the fear of God, so that when you do meet that person to whom you are attracted, God Himself might unite both hearts in indissoluble and true affection that will grow steadily and blossom into the deepest love. Pray now that you might be prepared for that moment.

There must be a seeking and praying period. May I ask you as a single man? What qualities is a Christian man to look for in a wife? I believe that the only beauty that can please a Christian man heart is one that is gentle, chaste, modest, economical, patient and careful of her husband's health. Such a person is whom I pray for you to have as your wife so that you may have a tremendous marital life that would turn out to be "Marriage a miracle of completion". Okay! You may say what then are the marks by which a godly and fit marriage partner may be identified? The Bible gave the characteristics of such virtuous woman in (Proverb 31:10-31.) If these virtues are to be found in a woman, then a woman should also be able to find them in the man. The three qualities that stand out in this chapter are as follows.

Firstly, the Bible describe a woman reputation as "A capable, intelligent, and virtuous woman—who is he who can find her? She is far more precious than jewels and her value is far above rubies or pearls." (Prov. 31:10.) This is to say that she is morally perfect and invaluable. You need to understand that, "Charm and grace are deceptive, and beauty is vain (because it is not lasting), but a woman who reverently and worshipfully fears the Lord, she shall be praised!" (Proverb 31:30.) Such a woman is from the Lord and so rare is this treasure that the challenge is given. "Who can find a virtuous woman?" They are not found everywhere; they have to be sought with great diligence and prayed for.

Abraham needs to send his servant to a distant land to find such a virtuous woman for his son. The first priority is not beauty, for this is a vain thing. The first priority is godly reputation. "A good name is rather to be chosen than great riches, and loving favor rather than silver and gold." (Prov. 22:1.) A good name and honor is more valuable than gold and riches. There must be that godly consistency and holiness of life. That is why Apostle Paul writes to Timothy that one who is godly will be adorned with good works. "But by doing good deeds (deeds in themselves good and for the good and advantage of those contacted by them), as befits women who profess reverential fear for and devotion to God." (1 Tim 2:10.) In fact, this passage is not condemning any one style, ornament, or garment, but demanding moderation in dress and behavior in general as women professing godliness.

Let virtue, not beauty be the primary object, set against the vanity of beauty for the true happiness connected with a woman that feared the Lord; and this is the solid basis for happiness. One old married man once said, "If I choose a woman for her beauty, I shall love her no longer than while that continues and then farewell at once both duty and delight. But if I love her for her virtues, then when all other sandy foundations fail, yet will my happiness and love remain entire." You have to tap into this wisdom and make it work for you, not just for today but for your future.

Secondly, consider her clothing, her appearance and envision the type of a wife she will become, for the Bible says, "Strength and dignity are her clothing and her position is strong and secure; she rejoices over the future (the latter day or time to come, knowing that she and her family are in readiness for it)" (Proverbs 31:25.) How many are deluded and deceived by these vainglorious appearances that have been pressed before us continually in this generation, where beauty and fashion are all that behold the eye?

An example of what I'm saying is the extravagance in ornament and costly garments that Apostle Peter rebukes that, "Let not yours be the (merely) external adorning with (elaborate) interweaving and knotting of the hair, the wearing of jewellery, or changes of cloth." (1 Peter 3:3.) Let not the outward adorning be the chief aim in your life, but let it be the hidden man of the heart, in that which is not corruptible, even the ornament of a meek and quiet spirit, which is in the sight of God of great price.

Thirdly, consider her conversation, "She opens her mouth in skillful and godly wisdom, and on her tongue is the law of kindness (giving counsel and instruction)." (Proverbs 31:26.) She opens her mouth in wisdom. Kindness is the grace of her lips. She is wise and intelligent and highly cultured in mind and manners. She is graceful and even-tempered in all her ways. Another example you have to know and emulate from the scriptures is, "When they observe the pure and modest way in which you conduct yourselves, together with your reverence (for your husband; you are to feel for him all that reverence includes: to respect, defer to, revere him—to honor, esteem, appreciate, prize, and in human sense, to adore him, that is, to admire, praise, be devoted to, deeply love, and enjoy your husband)." (1 Peter 3:2.)

I still believe there are excellent women who are not lords over their husbands, tyrants over their workers, and haughty toward their neighbors in this generation. The virtuous woman has not only the law of grace in her heart, but also wisdom in her mouth and kindness upon her tongue and an excellent example of a meek and quiet spirit. Her conversation is seasoned with grace. The unmarried person who seeks a marriage partner is to seek the conversation of one who is wise and kind, chaste and godly.

Beware of that unattached person who cannot speak of Christ and His unsearchable love. Keep well clear of entanglements with such people, whatever their profession of faith might be. Whether they have been baptized or not, beware of those who have carnal and worldly conversation. Seek out a partner whose conversation is pure, wholesome, godly and full of Christ.

If you want your marital relationship to be strong as "Marriage a Miracle of Completion" you must bring into the union spiritual understanding.

This is the secret for a successful marriage so that God can be in the centre of your relationship. You see, being kind to your spouse is a way of being obedience to the Word of God who created you and me to give pleasure to Him. Getting this mindset will give your marriage more meaning and ultimately more pleasure. This is a spiritual encouragement that you have to realize as a man or woman preparing for marital relationship. You must know and understand that marriage is not a business, social partnership or just a companionship but a spiritual bonding into oneness.

This is where you need to understand that without God in your marriage, you will only try but at the end of it all, things may not go the right way it should. Deep in the instincts of a human being, there is a bond between a man and a woman. The holy bond makes each member of the married couple part of one another and you have to understand that intimacy gives away a piece of you forever and that is why you need to be sure that the pieces you are giving away is to the right person with whom you want to share the rest of your life.

Choose right with the wisdom of God your future partner, so that you don't have a bad experience of marital life? It will be very hard to disengage, and when you do try to cover up for your partner unfaithfulness, it may be an uphill task; a lost battle before the battle even begins.

When you do get married, it will be hard to stay married because your partner will always compare you with others that he or she has had intimacy with before or during your courtship together. You may then appear to your spouse to lack qualities that others he or she has been with possess. You need to have a positive attitude within yourself because Satan uses modern ideas, technology, government of the day, and many other devices to deceive women to rob them of their home, marriage, peace of mind and their children.

The women league claims that a woman does not need a man in the home anymore, but I can tell you categorically this is the lie of the devil. A lot of homes and children life has been messed up due to the lie of the devil using certain organization as a tool to destroy families because the single parent cannot cope alone doing what is suppose to be done by the husband and wife. Many children are in gangs, on the street corners taking drugs, committing crimes and prostitution because there is no father figure at home as someone to look up to, or to teach them the right way to go.

The devil have blindfolded some women and made them to set their own standards as to what should be in the home but it is not just the boundaries of responsibilities in marriage that have become blurred, but the lies of Satan has also created loneliness. Don't get me wrong here if you are a single person and it is not a sin. What I am saying here is to those people that have been married before with children and the father has been driven out of the house due to the lie of the devil. Jesus said that one can decide to be single for the sake of the kingdom of God and not everyone has this gift as it has been said earlier. For those that have this gift, there is nothing wrong.

I can understand that there are people who choose not to marry for other reasons outside the will of God, for instance, those that want to keep their independence, career or for economic reasons, but the truth is that they are self-centered and do not want the responsibilities attached to marriage. These set of people are deceived by Satan who has made them objects of ridicule. I want you to understand that love is the greatest weapon to fight against anti-marriage forces because it never fails. "Love never fails". (I Corinthians 13:18.)

CHAPTER 9

Speak the Language of Blessing of Peace

You have to develop the habit of speaking the language of the blessing of peace into your life, your home, your spouse and your children. People actions and the word of their mouth make it difficult for the blessing of peace to work in their life as God promised. For the Bible says, "The Lord will give (unyielding and impenetrable) strength to His people; the Lord will bless His people with peace." (Psalms 29:11.) The blessing of peace is one of the most precious of God's treasures.

God desires us to walk in His peace, i.e. "And let the peace (soul harmony which comes) from Christ rule (act as umpire continually) in your hearts (deciding and settling with finality all questions that arise in your minds, in that peaceful state) to which as (members of Christ's) one body you were also called (to live). And be thankful (appreciative), (giving praise to God always)." (Colossians 3:15.)

You are to allow the peace of Christ to rule within your heart. There are many things which seek your attention, seeking to occupy your thoughts and your time. But you must allow the peace of God, the settled peace and rest of the Lord to continue in your heart. God desires to manifest His peace in your heart if you allow Him in all of your circumstances to be part of your life in order to manifest in every area.

God has promised us the blessing of peace i.e. to be at peace with Him, at peace with our self, and at peace with one another. It is the peace that God give in the midst of trying circumstances. God's peace can abide within us as our strength, a stabilizing force, the peace which is rooted in God's own presence within us. People in the world today are searching for something to give them peace; something that will bring them into contentment and rest, not realizing that peace, is the gift from God.

Jesus promise rest for our souls. He said, "Come to me, all you who labor and are heavy laden, and overburdened and I will cause you to rest. (I will ease and relieve and refresh your soul.) Take my yoke upon you, and learn of me, for I am gentle (meek) and humble (lowly) in heart, and you will find rest (relief and ease and refreshment and recreation and blessed quiet) for your souls. For my yoke is wholesome (useful, good—not harsh, hard, sharp, or pressing, but comfortable, gracious, and pleasant), and my burden is light and easy to be borne." (Matthew 11:28-30.)

Jesus invites us to come to Him. Those who are weighed down with burdens and cares are invited to come to Jesus and to receive rest in their souls. As we come to Jesus, and allow Him to rule within our hearts, we will find rest for our souls. As we allow Jesus to direct and guide our lives, we begin to come into His peace.

The problem with people is that many times we try to carry the burdens by our self. We try to carry the weight of problems and difficulties upon our shoulders, while Jesus is beckoning us to come to Him, to cast our burdens on Him, and to receive the blessing of peace. We must allow Him to carry our burdens. There are many things that Satan is using against you in his attempt to rob you of your peace.

Things like: (a) fear of the future (b) worry (c) fear of circumstances (d) conflicts with people (e) past failures (f) fear of what people may say or think about us (g) financial pressures. May I encourage you not to allow Satan to steal your peace, but start believing every promises of God for your situation from His Word, for your life? Let the peace of God be the treasure that you must guard, and keep within your hearts. The Lord has promised to bless you with peace, and you must not allow Satan to take it away.

Jesus promise you and me peace, when He said, "Peace I leave with you, my peace I give to you; not as the world gives, do I give to you. Let not your heart be troubled, nor let it be fearful." (John 14:27.) Jesus gave us a gentle command, when He said, "Let not your hearts be trouble." You need to learn not to allow the things around you to trouble your heart. But start to speak the language of the blessing of peace into every situation especially your marital life.

God created the whole earth by the word of His mouth. He said, "Let there be . . ." and there was (Genesis). God's words are powerful. You are made in the image of Him, so your word too is expected to be powerful. Let the word of your mouth bring the blessings of peace of God into your life, your marriage and your home. It is a good thing to cultivate the habit of speaking positive words of blessings of peace into your life and the people around you.

Hear what the Bible says, "A man shall be satisfied with good by the fruit of his mouth: and the recompense of a man's hands shall be rendered unto him." (Proverbs 12:14.) This is to say that a good man shall be satisfied with the fruit of his lips, and he will reap the good that he sows. I believe kind words, praise-living, living a holy life, caring, love and positive confession will enhance the rain of God's peace and blessing upon your marriage. Let your thoughts change from negative to positive, lack to abundance in every area of your life because out of the abundance of your heart, your mouth speaks.

Husband and wife that want to stay and enjoy the rest of their life together must learn to speak the language of peace and blessings to one another, their children, marriage, home, finances and everything around them. You have to understand that the words that come out of your mouths have creative power and abilities. "He who guards his lips guards his life but he who speaks rashly will come to ruin." (Proverb 13:3.)

You have to understand that the government of the tongue is commanded by God. We have two eyes and two ears to see and hear but we are to speak with one tongue fenced with the teeth. Hear what the Bible say that, "The tongue that brings healing is a tree of life but a deceitful tongue crushes the spirit." (Proverb 15:4.) Hard words, praise-living, living a holy life, caring/love and positive confession will enhance the rain of God's blessings. Let your language be of God because He is the author of positive confession.

The quality of your life depends on the word of your mouth. Let husband and wife control the words that come out of their mouths so that they can be all that God has promised them in scriptures. You must not underestimate the incredible force of your tongue. It is very true that our tongue cannot be controlled by human ability alone because the tongue is full of deadly poison. That is why every husband must know that the negative words from him could kill his marriage. It can be a continuous slow but constant flow of poison to his marriage.

I want you to learn from this story of a man, who killed his wife by poisoning her eye-liner. Every time the wife uses the eye-liner, a little poison enters into her body. This is the way negative words slowly destroys a marriage. The truth of the circle of everyone's life is continually excited by the tongue unless it is kept sanctified. Evil surmising, misrepresentation, falsehood, envying, wrath, and malice; all of these form part of the destroying flames of fire from the tongue of those that does not believe in the Word of God!

Although, the tongue is the least member of the body, but can bridle the whole body. There is nothing in this world that has been found in nature that can be comparing to the double use of the tongue (to bless or to curse) out of the same mouth. For comparison sake from nature: A fountain cannot produce sweet and sweet water at the same time. A fig tree cannot produce olives. A vine cannot produce figs likewise the ocean cannot produce sweet water.

This the reason why every husband has to understand that you cannot treat your wife badly and expect her to be the best wife you would cherish for the rest of your life. Husbands, learn not to criticize your wife, but use wisdom to encourage her all the time. And the wife should do like wise to her husband. God loves you and want you to love everyone especially your spouse.

In some relationships, husband and wife play the blaming game that is not helpful to their marriage and to the peace of their home and family. Let me ask you this question that how many times have you just tolerated your spouse? This is mainly common in men bullying their spouse physically and emotionally so that submission can be achieved but what you may not understand is that you are building resentment and inflicting hurt and fear in her. This is not the way to love your wife, and it is wrong to treat one another in such a way that is not glorifying God. This is an abuse, and you should pray for forgiveness and stop and make a turn around for a fresh start in treating your wife with the love of Christ.

One of the problems that are affecting many marriages is the lack of effective communication skills. Ineffective communication skill is when one or both spouses feel unappreciated, disregarded or disrespected. It always resulted in frequent fighting and misunderstanding in marriage. This brings about limitations in the relationship and none of the couple gets anything successful out of their marriage. You must eliminate negative mindset such as offense, bitterness, anger, resentment, disappointment and disloyal to your spouse if you want to experience a strong marital relationship.

The question really is? How can you handle the things you do not like that your spouse do? Truth be told, if you really love your spouse as you claimed you do and you want to have a lasting and successful marital relationship, then you have tell your spouse the truth in love and not in an angry outburst. You don't have to hide the truth from him or her and allow pressure to mount up that it will result into shouting and screaming at one another.

Remember that God created Eve to be Adam's help-meet. Adam would not have been completed, whole or fulfilled without Eve as the one God designed to complete him. I pray that as you read this book, the Almighty God, the creator of heaven and earth, will open your eyes of understanding for marital relationship that will make you grow and complete in love with your spouse without reservation. The scripture says that two people (husband and wife) (male and female) are better than one person, for when one falls, the other will lift him up.

I believe that good communication plays an important part in our everyday relationship, be it at home, work place or anywhere we go. The truth is that even in our relationship with God, good communication is vital and important too. The way we think, relate, communicate, the tone of our voice or our body language can break our home day in day out and this is often the practical reality of everyday living. Satan uses this aspect of lies, challenges and bad habits to destroy families from been together. The sad thing is that married couples assist the destroyer to achieve this objective of separation and divorce by not obeying God commandment for their marital life.

I want you to stop reading, sit back and think of your attitude and the way you answered your spouse the last time you have a misunderstanding. Search your heart right now and realize that only if you had exercised a little patience and keep quiet. The situation will not have turn badly as it was on that day. I know that it is very difficult and challenging when your mind is boiling for a fight. Just imagine if Jesus Christ were to come back at that very minute that you allowed your flesh, ego, and pride take control of you without giving the Holy Spirit any chance to take control of the situation.

You have to understand that the speech nerve centre has such power over the body system. Stop saying negative pronouncement against yourself, your home and your marriage? Such as (I'm going to divorce you sooner than you think). This is because whatever you pronounce, then right away, all the nerves receives that message and they say, "Oh, lets prepare to go for divorce, for we have received instructions from our central communication that we should prepare to go for divorce.

Then in natural sequence they adjust their physical attitude for every situation and circumstance to go for divorce. If a spouse keeps on saying, "I'm going to kill you one day" then right away all the nerves begin to declare the same thing. "Yes" they respond, we received instruction from the central nervous system saying that we are going to kill the spouse one day. We must prepare ourselves to kill the spouse one day.

You can experience a strong, lasting and successful marital life but you have to change your negative pronouncement of yourself, your spouse and your family because your conversation carried much meaning and authority than you may think. It always makes an impact in your life and all the people around you. Right now if you change your negative pronouncement to positive in every area of your life, things may get better by the grace of God.

I believe that you will make an important change to your marital life for a successful marriage. You have to stop speaking in a negative manner because like attracts like and since you act as if you are a negative minded person, you will always attracts negative things, negative thoughts, negative forces. And this attraction if it remains consistent will allow you to permanently dwell in unstable and unhappy relationship.

You may be wondering whether God really sees how you are being bullied or abused. Yes, God sees everything you are going through, just hold on and He will take you to an expected end. God knows and sees you more than you think and He sees your situation even before it happened. That is why you need to speak at all times the language of blessing of peace every day to have a "marriage, a miracle of completion."

CHAPTER 10

All in the Family

I robustly believe that the family unit is the measurement of true and rewarding success in life. How a man is conducting his affairs and that of his family directly or indirectly relates to how successful he is in other areas of his life. For example, if a man is successful in the business world but does not have the respect of his family, he is not a man of integrity. He is a failure and an unsuccessful being. Let me encourage you today that it is not too late for any man to sit back and make correction in whatsoever way he may have let down his wife and children.

For anyone who chooses worldly success, selfishness, covetousness over the well-being of his or her family, needs to pray for forgiveness and make amendment before it is too late. Each person knows deep down inside, the decision taken, that led to the disintegration of his whole family, is not of God. If amendment is made today, your offspring will not have to pay the costly price of your wrong decision to separate or divorce your spouse.

The reasons why youths of these days have no respect for the law or nobody else is because there is no role model at home they can look up to as a father figure. Father figure at homes nowadays is becoming a thing of the past and this is making many youths destiny to be aborted. As a parent, you need to have the habit of confessing the Word of God in faith over your children daily because the word of your mouth has tremendous creative power.

The Bible says that life and death are in the power of the tongue. The moment a word comes out of your mouth, you have given birth to it. This is a spiritual principle and it works whether what you say is good or bad (negative or positive). Remember God created the heavens and the earth with His word. As parents, we have the responsibility before God and man to train, orient and encourage our children to make the right choices. When they misbehave or disobey the authority God placed on them, they should be corrected and disciplined in love.

Your children should see that you love God and are god-fearing. As a parent myself, I believe that the words I use on my children have the capacity and the power to mold and shape their future as I sow the right seeds of blessings and faith into their life. So, you need to start speaking positive words into the life of the people around you i.e. your husband or wife including your children, extended family members and friends if you want them to turn living the best. This is one of the reasons why husband and wife must stop cursing one another. Many husband and wife say negative things to one another and they become each other's worst enemy at home. This is totally wrong and it should stop immediately.

I believe that you want your children to be productive and successful in life, then start declaring the promises of God into their life and their future rather than cursing and swearing at them. With the words of your mouth, you may bless or curse. Let every father understands that your child came out of your loins, and he or she is part of you. Likewise every mother must do what it takes so that your children become one of the best around for the glory of God. The Bible says that, children are a blessing from the Lord. As a parent you possess the spiritual authority and have the ability to bring success, prosperity and good health into the present and future of your children.

Frequently, parents in particular mothers slip into being harsh and use hard words on their children and find faults like, "Why can't you be the best in your class?", or "Go and clean your room, it looks like an unattractive place!", or "You cannot do anything right in your life." Let me encourage mothers to must realize that all these negative confessions day-in, day-out may cause their children to lose confidence and self-value.

You must be careful not to speak words of discouragement to your children so as not to dishearten them and destroy their self-image. You need to realize that a verbally-abused child will have insecurity as well as inferiority complex and he or she will always think that he or she will amount to nothing. Many adults still suffer from the negative words spoken to them when they were young.

You need to know that every negative word sown into your children's life may be a curse on them now and in their future. God placed you as a blessing to your children and not a curse and remember that God will hold you responsible if you destroy their destiny. Isaac blessed Jacob instead of Esau, but when Esau came to receive his own blessing from their father as the first born, it was already too late.

Esau insists that his father should bless him but Isaac's answer was insightful and powerful: **No, he said, the words have already gone forth and I cannot take them back. I said** Jacob will be blessed and he will always be blessed. Isaac gave Esau a less significant blessing, but it was not as significant and powerful as the first blessing he gave to Jacob that he took to be the first born. Isaac used all his will, might and soul to bless Jacob such that nothing could stand in the way of the blessing and it just has to manifest.

You have to remember the case of Isaac, Jacob and Esau every time you are provoked so that you do not voice out negative words to any of your children or your spouse when you are angry. Take timeout to think and allow the Holy Spirit to intervene, so that you do not destroy the destiny of your children or your family by the negative words spoken out by you. Rather bless your children always and encourage them to follow the way of the Lord.

Remember that whatever comes out of your mouth whether positive or negative, you will not be able to retrieve it back because words are like an egg. When it is broken, it can never be put back together. What you must understand is that it is not easy to control the tongue when one is angry. Always remember that once words are uttered, they take on a life of their own. May I encourage you today to begin to let the words of your mouth be a blessing to your family especially your spouse and children and not a curse.

Let's pray . . .

Thank you Lord Jesus for blessing me with a family! I pray that these blessing will continue to overflow as I continuously rely on you. I repent today of saying negative words to myself, my spouse and my children and I ask for your forgive. I submit my tongue and my heart to you; for the Bible says that out of the abundance of the heart the mouth speaks.

So teach me Lord to speak positive words of blessing from my heart to my spouse and my whole family and lead me in the path of righteousness and peace in every area of my life in Jesus name. Amen.

CHAPTER 11

Godly Offspring

Regardless of the way you interpret this passage, you have to comprehend it to be a blessing. "And this you do with double guilt; you cover the altar of the Lord with tears (shed by your unoffending wives, divorced by you that you might take heathen wives), and with (your own) weeping and crying out because the Lord does not regard your offering any more or accept it with favor at your hand.

Yet you ask why does He reject it? Because the Lord was witness (to the covenant made at your marriage) between you and the wife of your youth, against whom you have dealt treacherously and to whom you were faithless. Yet she is your companion and the wife of your covenant (made by your marriage vows).

And did not God make (you and your wife) one (flesh)? Did not one make you and preserve your spirit alive? And why (did God make you two) one? Because He sought a godly offspring (from your union)! Therefore take heed to yourselves, and let no one deal treacherously and be faithless to the wife of his youth. For the Lord, the God of Israel says; I hate divorce and marital separation and him who cover his garment (his wife) with violence.

Therefore keep a watch upon your spirit (that it may be controlled by My Spirit that you deal not treacherously and faithlessly (with your marriage mate.)" (Malachi 2:13-16.) In this case, you will end with approximately the same conclusion: The practice condemned by Malachi—such as divorce is incompatible with godliness.

The truth here expresses God's hatred of divorce i.e. putting away. Let not anyone with intelligence act that way; for what did that one do, who was seeking offspring from God? So watch out for your feelings so that you do not be unfaithful to the wife of your youth. You have to understand the consequences divorce will have on your whole family! Not only does it destroy the relationship between husband and wife and the family, it may also destroy one's relationship with God.

God tell us that He hate Divorce. He compares it to covering one's self with violence—wearing violence like clothing. In the scripture, God warned us that as long as we continued to do this, he would totally ignore our religious behaviour—activities we thought were pleasing to Him.

Let me remind you that there are financial and spiritual consequences that go with divorcing your spouse. This "faith-breaking" conduct has an impact that goes beyond one's relationship with your spouse. The scripture says that it can even affect the relationship of one's *offspring* with God. Although there is no guarantee that the offspring of *non-divorced* parents will always be *godly*, or that the offspring of *divorced* parents will always be *ungodly*, this passage shows us that the willingness of a parent to do what God *hates* (divorce) has a profound impact on the offspring of that now-broken union. So what is your conclusion in this matter?

You may be unsure before now about the meaning of divorce and the consequences that goes beyond the husband and wife? You may, or may not like some of the things the Bible is saying concerning divorce. But certain things have already been revealed, if you are willing to accept them. And though you may have difficulties in understanding some parts of the book of Malachi about divorce, but by the time you get to the end of it, you will discover that your moral obligation to obey the commandment of God not to divorce is very clear.

What I want you to understand is that the Word of God made it very understandable that God hate divorce. To bring up godly offspring, husband and wife need to stay together as a specific moral obligation. It does not deny the possibility that *genuine* repentance might lessen the impact of some of the consequences that occur when this moral obligation is violated. However, I want you to remember that sin *does* have consequences that repentance *cannot* remove. Even if you repent and are eternally forgiven, there may still be consequences you have to endure in this present life. There may also be long-term (and perhaps eternal) consequences that affect others due to your disobedience to the Word of God.

Every parent should know and understand that the reason why their children must obey them comes from the commandment of God, and from a place of love and respect instead of fear. As a parent, you need to share your life stories with your children so that they would understand that their parents has lived through many stages of life, survived numerous errors, endured hardships and broken hearts, which no books could begin to equip them with the education obtained by trial and error of life. Therefore, let your children understand that when you guide them away from harm, it is done so as an act of love. Let your children understand that you feel their hurts and you attempt to spare them the pain.

I feel for parents nowadays because technology is playing such a huge role in today's children environment. So encourage them to use it wisely so that it does not be a strong hold in their life. Children nowadays expect rapid responses and results in whatever they do. Materialism is more prevalent in this generation than it was in their parents. In many families the old stories beginning with, "When I was your age . . . ," and these and that! I believe many parents can relate to this. But you need to stop using this emphasis on your children because that is your generation, and this is their generation. No parent ever prays for their children to go through whatever they (the parents) may have gone through in life.

This is what I need to say to every parent that respect is one the secret for a strong marriage. It begins with respecting yourself and your spouse. Your children are observing every situation, even if they don't approve or disapprove of it. Think back to your childhood and your observation of your parents. How they allow themselves to be treated badly in relationship that is suppose to be model for the children to emulate. How they dress; what places are they frequent whether church or otherwise; who were their friends; did they job hop or maintain same job and what role did faith play in their lives? I believe these all add up to self-respect. You learned through observing your parents and your children will do likewise.

As a father or mother, you need to know and understand that the word "obey" is demanding, whereas "respect" is more natural. Children similar to adults crave praise, acceptance, understanding and then being listened to! Remember when you are your children's ages, can you somehow identify with their age about your thoughts, feelings, attitudes, needs and dislikes? This reminiscence will enable you to finding the middle ground, listen to current trends and get a feel for the world in which your children walk.

Do you recall when you are a young man who wore baggy trousers or doing some crazy stuff back then? Or can you recall when you are a young woman with gobs of makeup and hairspray? So today, children wants to wear brand new jeans purchased with holes in them or wear nice new trainers matching their outfits. They pierce body parts we wouldn't dream of or piercing and decorate their body with tattoos in the name of fashion. What can you as parents do so that your children don't copy the wrong fashion like piecing and decorating their body with tattoos?

I want you as a parent to ask your children this question, "Are you respecting your self"? Or can you picture Grandma or grandpa with tattoo on the back of his or her neck! That's how you will look at grandma or grandpa age if you decorate your body with tattoo. This is simple statement that without lecture or pressure will go a long way. I want you to understand that there is a way to communicate the right words to your children to encourage them now and in their future.

Sorry to say, it often takes a serious illness or death of a parent or grandparent before some children begin to recognize the depth of the love that person had for him or her. At that point, memories of what (parent or grand parent) of that person was relaying to the child become significant. All you can do for your children is to be present at the moment, accept them, love them, encourage them and praise their attempts regardless of the result. The evidence that they obey may not be as evident as you may wish, but it will make itself known at some point.

The commandment to obey your father and mother is non negotiable. "To many youths of this generation, these words sound like something out of the dark ages. The command to honour your parents "(which includes willing submission and obedience)" comes from God, and He attaches the following incentive to heed this commandment. (That it may go well with you and you may endure a long time on the earth.) "Honour thy father and mother, (which is the first commandment with promise) that it may be well with thee, and thou mayest live long on the earth." (Ephesians 6: 2-3.)

The stakes is high and so let us take a fresh look at what honouring your father and mother really mean. What "Honouring" them means? "Honour" involves recognizing duly constitute authority. For instance, Christians are commanded to "have honour for the king." (1 Peter 2:17.) While you may not always agree with a national ruler, his position or office is still to be respected.

In the same way, God has vested parents with certain authority over their children. That means that your children must accept you (their parents) as their God given authority over them on this earth, to direct and nurture in the right way of the Lord. It may be true that other parents may be lenient than you in discipline their children, but you as a parents have the responsibility of deciding what is best for your children. You have to let your children know and understand that honoring their parents also means accepting correction, not sulking or throwing tantrums when it is administered? Your children need to know that only a fool "disrespects the discipline of his father." (Proverbs 15:5.)

Let me encourage you of how to deal with bitterness, no matter who you are? It is a spirit that needs to be eliminated quickly unless it will spread like cancer if not remove as soon as possible. One thing you should understand is to stay calm because being angry accomplishes nothing; neither does hateful and unpleasant behaviour. For the Bible warns that you should, "Take care that rage does not allure you into spiteful [actions] . . . Be on your guard that you do not turn to what is hurtful." (Job 36:18-21.)

One of the reasons why children should obey their parents is that God commanded them to do so. There is no negotiation or any compromise whether they should or they shouldn't. One thing you should let your children know is that there are blessings for obedience and there are curses for disobedience too. Children should be taught to obey their parents from their early stage of life because it is the responsibility of all parents to teach their children the way they should go. Children need to learn respect, honesty, fairness, what is right and what is wrong, including good manners from home.

If you don't teach your children obedience at an early stage of their life, they may turn out to be disobedient person throughout their entire life. They will not want to obey anyone and they will think they are above the law in all things until they have a rude awakening but it may be too late to change then. Take for example your pet dog. If you don't teach your pet dog how to behave around your children and what the dog is allowed to do or not allowed to do; the dog will one-day bite your children and chew up everything in the house. The dog may end up attacking you too.

Each person has to learn that he or she cannot do as he or she so choose and abide by his/her own rules to survive in life. You have to teach your children that there are rules and regulations that all mankind must adhere to, and if they don't, they will be placed in an institution where they will not be able to be around the public until they learn how to obey and respect other people. I believe the reason we have so much "wild" disrespect youths in our society today is because they have not been taught properly how to obey their parents, other people and the authority from their early age.

One of the reasons for youth disobedience is that some parents work all day and when they come home, have no time for their children. They are busy with different things while their children is hanging around the street corners until late hours and go to bed when they so choose. Their children have no constraint of when to come home or when to go to bed. Their parents are not teaching them what is right or wrong, and they are left to make their own decisions and rules at an early age on a daily basis. These children are more or less raising themselves and this may be an issue for them in the near future to obey any authority over them.

Some children may not be held responsible of their actions because they have not been taught how to obey and how to act in a proper manner. They will become the same type of dysfunctional people as their parents when they have a family because they were never taught any type of rules and regulations to adhere to in their life. It's a sad situation because what we end up seeing in our society is these adults who have never been taught what obedience are, and what they were expected to do in their young life. I believe it is the parent's responsibility to look after children.

Children need to be nurture, care for, love and show the right way to follow so that they do not go the wrong path of destruction. No greater gift in life can a child give their parents than love and obedience. Obedience shows respect and honor for the life given to them. It isn't always easy to obey, since the inclinations of our heart stems from imperfect beings, but children can obey their parents to the best of their ability.

Let me encourage you as a parent reading this book that obedience in a child, who lives at home where his or her needs are met, is the key to a successful adult life when he or she leave home. In life, we all have rules and regulation we have to follow to live a trouble free lifestyle. So, every parent has been given an important role to instill discipline in their children and everything needed to become responsible adult to themselves and the society in general. The truth of discipline your children is that you are giving them the tools to succeed in life. It is based on building the right relationship with your children more than using any techniques. By discipline them, you are developing their inner control that last a lifetime.

The reality is that you will test the very fiber of your children's patience many times; you might come across to them many times and bruise their egos. Most times, your dedication that wants the best for your children might come across as harsh, rather than an act of love! Reminding your children that there might be times they will not fully understand why you as their parent are treating them the way you do; this can help them in that moment to obey your wishes, despite their desire to rebel against your discipline.

You have to understand that as children grow older, the need for obedience is needed. More disagreements seem to arise, as do misunderstanding. Of course, these pre-teen years and teenage years are full of varying degrees of ever changing hormones. They believe that you as their parents know nothing, but their friends know it all. It's good to help them to appreciate that you have far more experience in life and you're trying to direct them in a way that is for their wellbeing. While their friends might be able to relate to the hormone shifts, they cannot fully give sound advice that will ensure their safe course through those tumultuous years.

It is true that not all homes have parents who impart good values and manners into their children, but despite this, obedience must be learned. The importance of obedience to parents is stipulated in the Bible that, "Children, obey your parents in the Lord (as His representatives), for this is right. Honor (esteem and value as precious) your father and your mother—this is the first commandment with a promise." (Ephesians 6:1-3.) And the promise that God says to those that obey this commandment of obedience to parents is for long life.

Hear what the Bible say, "Regard (treat with honor, due obedience, and courtesy) your father and mother that your days may be long in the land the Lord your God gives you." (Exodus 20:12.) While some do not believe in the Bible, but the principles of this commandment is beneficial to everybody, no matter which race or color you may be.

Life is a precious gift; and it is you the parents that give it. You are the ones responsible for "training up your children in the way they should walk." So compliance to you as their parent is your children gift of appreciation for their life. Your children come into your life as precious gifts. You need to raise them to be all that they can be and to accomplish many things in their life. In order to be able to guide them and lead them on the right path, they need to respect and teach them the things that are right and wrong. Your children need you to help them develop a good sense of moral and the code of ethics to live by.

Your children need to obey you as their parents because you have the power to teach them lessons that help them ready to face any situation in the future. The truth is that if a child doesn't respect or obey the parents, that child will not respect or obey anyone including the authority. Children have to learn that there are certain consequences to things they do whether positive or negative and they need to learn the lessons from it. You as a parent have the upper hand in making your children obey you and take control and not your children control you.

You must understand that when your children obey you as their parents and listens to you, it creates a stronger bond between you and them. They will be able to handle situations on their own better and consider the outcome of what they do by what they have learned from you as their father or mother. You must understand that when you don't take control but let your children run wild at a young age, you can expect the same behavior when they gets older. There will be no respect, no good judgments, and poor common sense. I want every parent to understand that for your children obeying you as their parents is fundamental in their development. From parents, a child tends to learn so much about life, manners and rules. These lessons prepare them for school, work, and dealing with peers. It also gives them guidelines to follow when they become parents themselves and prepares them for the things to come.

This is an example; being in a store or restaurant and seeing someone kids running all over the place, yelling, and screaming is a sign of lack of discipline of those children. There is no reason why parents can't have control over their children to obey their instruction other than being lazy themselves. One of the reasons why your children must obey you is by enforcing the consequences and sticking to what you say you are going to do. Every child needs guidance and need to learn respect.

It is your duty as parents to make this happen and to help your children grow into people that are going to be upstanding members of the society. If they don't obey, don't be afraid to take action. Losing television privileges or x-box isn't going to hurt them one bit. For you as a parent not taking control and making your children obey and learn respect can hurt them in the long run and create bigger headaches for you in the near future. I believe when children obey their parents, their life will falls into balance, harmony and lead to a better and more productive lifestyle.

I believe obedience and love are the greatest virtue and must be instilled in the little minds. Your children must be taught to obey their parents and the authority right from the time they are able to understand right from wrong. You must always remember that you are doing the right thing when you ask your children to obey you. You need to let your children understand that obedience to parents will prevent them from harm. If you love your child enough, you will definitely make sure that your child carries out many of your instructions.

Say for example, you repeatedly warn your child not to play with a knife because he or she may end up injuring him or herself. Frequently, children learn the hard way. Telling a child not to play with fire or a flame will save the child's life. Training your child to obey in practical ways and explaining the pros and corns of disobedience is very helpful for good upbringing.

Let me encourage every parent today to be strict in love when it comes to making your children to be restraint and obey you. Setting up rules in your family and getting your children to understand the rules is important. You have to let them understand that breaking any rule, there will be consequence that may follow. Once the rules are laid down, and then it will help your children to understand that mum and dad are serious and mean what they say. They should understand that obedience will makes them avoid problems and any serious danger.

This is another level of your children life when they are near marriageable age; you should start praying for them that God will establish a Christian home for each one of them. Pray for them so that the Holy Spirit may lead and take control of situation of things that they will get God's choice of wife or husband. I know that raising godly children and replenish the earth is one of the reasons God created the marriage institution. God has given the duty of raising children to parents, and not to the government, the school, the television sets or the society at large to have godly offspring.

Many parents have abandoned their responsibility of bringing up their children to complete strangers. This explains why modern day youths lack discipline and tolerance. Let every parent stand up for the truth of the Word of God that moral foundation of a child has to start from home. The Bible says that, "if you refuse to discipline your children, it proves you don't love them; if you love your children, you will be prompt to discipline them." (Proverbs 13:24.) Furthermore, "Discipline your children while there is hope. If you don't, you will ruin their lives." (Proverbs 19:18.) The Bible give us parents a clear instruction that "To discipline and reprimand a child produces wisdom, but a mother is disgraced by an undisciplined child" (Proverbs 29:15.)

Parents need to show good examples to their children as to emulate so that they will be seen and heard. The Bible does not support child abuse but you should teach your children to know how to tidy up as a regular routine; how to keep safe and clean their toys and playing materials, eating and other personal things. This will help them to be able to take care of themselves when you are not there to help them.

It is good for parents not to bribe their children with money to do or for doing housework as this may rob them of their self-esteem. Children should be assigned some duties and responsibilities around the house to prepare them for the future. It gives them a sense of belonging and will help them to become better adults. You need to teach your children how to save and invest money from their early age. They should be taught how to keep and manage a bank account of their own and should be given the opportunity of withdrawing regularly a certain amount of money as their pocket money. You should monitor how your children spend their money wisely.

It is true that the habits and manners of parents get passed to their children. That is why you should therefore be very careful as your children are watching and will surely copy whatever you do one day. A man who beats his wife or commit adultery should not be surprised if his son or daughter does the same thing when he or she grows up. This is a warning to husbands not to beat his wife or to have a mistress on the side but to love his wife as Christ love the church. Likewise to wives to stop disrespecting and foul mouth her husband but to love and respect him as a service to the Lord. Stop comparing your husband to another man and stop living adulterous lifestyle because your daughter or son will do the same thing.

Let your children be loved so that they will be always ready to share their troubles with you as their parents and not with their mate or strangers who may mislead them. As a parent you shouldn't react in anger or in violence when your children make mistake if you want them to trust you and confide in you and not in a strangers. You should always encourage them to believe in themselves and rely on God too.

Pray frequently for them and work with them to develop positive thinking ability from their tender age to encourage them in the Word of God that will help them to believe that, with God all things are possible. Help them in directing their minds towards positive and not negative thoughts all the time that create fear, discouragement and depression.

Let parents pray specifically for the salvation of their children if they have not accepted the Lord Jesus Christ as their personal Lord and Saviour. I want you to know that salvation is an experience with God alone and not with any Church, organization, friends or denomination. Taking your children to church alone is not enough to guarantee their salvation but each child must have a personal relationship and commitment with the Lord Jesus Christ.

The truth is that the salvation of any parent cannot save their children. Each child needs to accept the Lord Jesus Christ as Lord and personal saviour and allow the Holy Spirit to do his regeneration work in him or her. You need to encourage your children to have the habit of reading the Word of God daily (Bible.) Hear what the Bible say, "Teach a child in the way that he should go and when he grows he will not depart from it"

(Proverb 22:6.) Have this understanding today, that the Spirit of God does nothing without the Word of God.

Teach your children to obey God and serve Him with all their heart and might to live a life of love just as Christ lived and gave himself up as a sacrifice for our sin. As I have said before that whatever you do, your children are watching your acts and behaviour and may copy them. So, do not participate in immoral acts, obscenity, foolish talk or coarse jokes that are out of place, backbiting, bitterness or resentment.

It is a good habit to teach your children to appreciate themselves, their parents, friends, and especially everything God does for them. As godly parents, pray for your children daily and stand in the gap for them so that they can enjoy everything God has ordained for them in life to become godly offspring.

CHAPTER 12

Encouraging Your Children to Bring Out the Best in Them

Let me inspire you today so that you can encourage your children to a heart to heart talk about life generally, especially in the area of sex that many family don't want to talk about. This is not only for parents alone but anyone that is in the position to encourage youths in the right manner that God want. This go to youth pastors too to say the truth about sex to youths in church to abstain from sex until they get marry. Parents and youth pastors have to educate the youth in our churches that they have no business about sex until they get married.

Nowadays, sex education is taught in schools but it is corrupting young minds and this brings problems to them now and later in their future. Truth be told, everyone need to understand that you can use protection in the physical realm to avoid being pregnant or catching disease but what about your spirit man? You cannot protect your spirit man with any other protection than abstain from sex and living in holiness for the Lord, if you are not married and that is fornication.

To parents and youth pastors, you shouldn't allow any more issue of sex cover-up to our youths in churches as the great mystery thing. The truth is if parents or the church don't deal with this issue truthfully, the now society will teach and encourage our youths the wrong thing about sex. Every youth pastors and parents in the church need to understand that lack of adequate information to church teenagers about sex before marriage will inspire and intrigue them to become more appealing. We know as parents that the lure of the unknown consumes the mind, just like Eve then regrets will set in after one taste of what you are not suppose to do now in the first place.

Let me encourage parents to teach their teenager children about sex education, first at home and not to see it as a taboo mentioning of it in the right perspective. If you ignore to teach them the right way, strangers will teach them wrongly. The consequences will be for you to deal with at the end of the day. You need to encourage your youths to adopt what is called "TRUE LOVE WAITS" contract. This contract has to be renowned every year and your teenagers will have to dutifully signs cards and pledges to wait for true love until they get married.

This is for every parent to understand that "True Love Waits" challenges your teenagers if they adopt it to make a commitment to sexual abstinence until marriage. It encourages moral purity by obedience to Biblical principles. It will utilize positive peer pressure if they adopt this system of holy living by making commitment to refrain from pre-marital sex and they too will be able to challenge their peers to do the same. These believe is base on the Word of God that requires teenagers and youths to be faithful to one's husband or wife, even before marriage.

You teenager may adopt the *True Love Waits pledge, which states*: "Believing that true love waits, I make a commitment to God, myself, my family, my friends, my future mate and my future children to be sexually abstinent from this day until the day I enter a biblical marriage relationship." In addition, True Love waits promote sexual purity, which encompasses not only abstaining from intercourse before marriage, but also abstaining from sexual thoughts, sexual touching, pornography, and actions that are known to lead to sexual arousal.

In our churches these days, many young men and women could have been protected if they have been told that sex is not some guilty pleasure denied them, but rather a part of God's plan for their future marriage and well worth the wait. Many babies could have been saved if only these young girls had realize not just the negative consequence of sex out of marriage but the positive truth of God about sex within marriage. You should love your children unconditionally irrespective of whether they behave nicely or not.

Your love for your children must go beyond their surface behaviours and it should bring out the best in them. They will feel this love and each day should not pass without your telling them that you love them. This will give them the courage to go out and be the best that God wants them to be. You should speak and act in ways that will give your children a positive self-image, believe in them and their potentials. It is a good thing for you to be role models for the traits and qualities you want your children to develop. Children know what their parents do and they can learn from them and their experience. So you must identify what is unique in each child and understand how to encourage him or her when challenges come.

Parents need to give positive remarks as well as support and then focus on the end result that is best for their children. You must think on your toe and speak out in the wisest possible way especially when your child messes up. Create time and make it a habit to read good books to your children especially when they are still young or if they are teenagers, spend quality time with them as much as possible. Every parent has to understand that life is a continuous seminar in character development, so you have to develop your children mentally, physically and spiritually.

You should offer gratitude to God frequently in the presence of your children and encourage them to thank God for everything. As a parent, pray that God grant you supernatural ability to evaluate events in a realistic positive way and ask your teenager children questions like "What will be a positive way of looking at this?" Or "How can we go from this to that? You must not forget that nobody is perfect especially when your children make mistakes then you need to help them learn from their mistakes. You must develop yourself as a parent to become better listener, better communicator and in other area of parenthood so that your children may be one of the best as God ordained.

Your children are your offspring, the joy of your today and your hope of tomorrow. You must love, protect, discipline and nurture them always in the right way. They must be encouraged not to give up on things easily especially things that are beneficiary to their future well being. You never know some day; your children may take care of you in your old age. You should be approachable and open to your children and attention must be giving to the signals from them. Every parent must understand that each child is unique, so there is no single approach to dealing with children. I believe a talk with an eight-year-old boy should be different from a fourteen-year-old girl or a fifteen-year-old boy.

You must teach your children to respect them self and others for this should start from their tender age. I know that children who get into the habit of speaking rudely and disrespecting his or her parents will find it harder respecting other people. It will be very challenging to learn good manners and way of life when older. You need to allow your children to do house work, such as cleaning their room or washing up their plates after eating and at times giving you a glass of water to drink. I believe such household tasks can not kill them but prepare them for their own good in the future.

The heartbreaking thing about children of these days is that parents are so busy serving them but their children don't know what it means to serve parents and others. May I encourage you to teach your children good manners such as when you get back home or any visitor come to your house, they should stop whatever they may be doing and welcome you or the visitor that come to your house. This is one of the manners you need to instill into your children when they are still living with you at home.

It will give you peace of mind in the future to teach your children good manners now while they are still young to serve as models of good behaviours to other children to follow. Let every father that are still at home help his wife instill discipline into their children, such as when she arrive home with shopping bags in her hands or still in the car by saying things like this; "mom's home, let's go and help her with the shopping bags and put them where they are suppose to be." I believe your eagerness as a father to help your wife will set a good example for your children to do the same whenever their mum comes home with shopping bags even when you are not around.

Similarly to every wife; if you are on the phone and your husband walks in from work or just coming from somewhere, you can say to the other person at the other end of the phone! Sorry, my husband just walk in, I have to go; I will call you later. This is a good way of showing respect and appreciation to your husband and it goes a long way. You are modeling a good wife habit to your husband by giving him honour as the head of your family and at the same time telling the other person on the phone that you are a good wife with good manners that have respect for your husband.

The most important thing is that your children will see respect between their father and mother and will copy what they see. What I want every parent to understand is that those who respect and help one another as husband and wife are tend to stay together no matter what they may be going through. And the husband and wife who try not to argue in the presence of their children are much more likely to have children who give respect to themselves and others. Whenever the mother is busy, the father should get the children to render a helping hand. For example, when the mother is washing the dishes then the father can help by participating in the chore himself. Then the children will see it that they too must help their mother in the household tasks.

You should be unyielding not to rush or respond to your child calling you every time from another room unless it is in an emergency, which you can recognize immediately for you to go to him or her. It is not a good home training for you to rush to your child every time to find out what he or she want. But let your child come to you when he or she is in need of anything. Educate your child or children a few times, and then if it happens again, just do not respond that child.

You should understand that your children will come to you if they want something urgent or important. Try as much as possible to avoid your child having argument with you whether at home or outside of your home as this promote lack of respect. Once you start to argue with your children, you have lost every control and ability to bring them up properly. Having a discussion that involves difference of opinion is okay, but an argument is not.

CHAPTER 13

Good Manners and True Education Begin At Home!

Every parent must understand that their children good manners have to start from home and not from the school as lots of people assumed. I believe it is the responsibility of parents or guardian to set good standard of discipline and pattern of behaviours of their children from home and not the teachers at school. Whatever standard of discipline a child has been train from home is the standard that the child will be encourage at school and not the other way round. Think about of it and ask yourself! Why it is that certain child receive suspension or expels from school, if not because of that child bad behaviour and lack of discipline from home.

The truth is that the child has not received any home training from his or her parents or guardian. The lack of home training causes a child to misbehave in the class room or in the school compound, and then the school authority will have no choice than to suspend or expel such child. The school authority cannot tolerate indiscipline and bad behaviours from any student because such bad behaviour may corrupt other students or cause problem for them in the school compound. You must understand that the educational system nowadays or the government cannot train your child or children with good manners and godly education but it is your responsibility as a parent to do so.

You can truthfully teach your child or children good manners and godly education. For the Bible says, "Teach your children to choose the right path, and when they are older, they will remain upon it." (Proverb

22:6.) This is an unfailing law that when your child is old enough to stay on it comes; he or she will do so. Guide your child with Godly instructions and direction on how to perform his or her duties, how to escape danger, and how to appropriate the blessings on the way. Teach these lessons deep into your child soul and lead him or her to practice them until they are part of his or her life and nature. Bath your child in prayer daily and instill the fear of God into him or her; assuredly your child will not depart from it.

May I say this with complete humility that every parent should watch out their own behaviour too? This is because what a child see all the time, the child imitate. It is proven that if a child is loud and plays rough, that child follows suit of the mother or father most of the time. What really astonish me is that most parents that fail to discipline their children put the blame on the school system and the government, and everyone else but not themselves.

Likewise, if a mother or the father is gentle, kind and patient, then their example will exercise a subtle influence on even the nosiest of any of their children. It is not only the mother or the wife that is responsible for the children's manner from home, but everyone at home because this made a lot of difference in raising responsible children. Let's put it this way; to be polite and gentle is part of the deal that must not be ignored to raise a family that in many years to come, you will not be feeling shame of your children.

I believe that you can train your children to be gentle, polite, have good manners, self-control under provocation and to do the daily practice of those small acts of self-denial, true courtesy, which do so much towards preparing them for the life ahead from their tender age. If you don't discipline your child or children today, you will regret it tomorrow because it will be too late to do then. You don't want to be frequent in court house due to your child committing crime or the police phoning you up in the middle of the night or coming to your house and wake you up in the night time because of your child involvement in crime or gang related issues.

I know that there is a way out if you can step up your disciplinary measure in love to communicate with your child in a language that he or she understand that relate more to your child level. As a parent, you have to understand that there is foolishness and silliness that are born in every child but there is a remedy for this as the Bible says "A youngster's heart is filled with foolishness, but discipline will drive it away."(Proverb 22:15.)

To begin with, there is basic manner training that parents should teach their child from home such as, waiting his or her turn and not interrupting other people when talking. This is to let your child understand that no one can hear if there are too many voices at once and should make the child understand to wait until someone talking is done. Then your child should be encouraged to ask his or her question and you should give your full-undivided attention so as not to undermine your child self-esteem.

There are basic home training that your child needs to be taught such as to greetings and appreciation. For instance when a visitor comes to your house, but this depends on the level of formality or familiarity and depending on your culture and ethics, you must teach your child or children to shake hands with adults who come over to your house, but it's not necessary to shake hands with other children but it is good to say "hello or hi" so that the visitor feels welcome.

Furthermore, you should teach your child or children basic manners such as to always say "please" and "thank you" to others especially those people that are older than them. This show respect and gratitude on the side of your child and in the event of receiving complement; it should be taken courteously. For example, if someone praises your child; teach him or her to be gracious and say "thank you" and avoid putting him or herself down or pointing out flaws. I believe true education starts from home, as parents must insist on their children to learn how to clean up or tidy up after themselves whether at home, at a friend's house or at school. Always let your children understand that any mess they made should be cleaned up.

The truth is that if any parent, be it the father or the mother withholds discipline from their child hates that child but the parent who corrects in love and trains their child has their child future at heart. You have to understand that training your child with good manners and true education is a lifetime benefit to use every day and make good impression on him or she and others be at home, school, work place or anywhere your child goes.

Good manners and true education I'm talking about is more than opening doors and writing "thank you" notes. Don't get me wrong here but opening door for others and writing "thank you" notes is good, but true courtesy goes deeper than that. I will like every parent to tap into this understanding that being polite and courteous means considering how others feel.

These means that you are showing the people around you that you are different positively by considering their feelings and respecting them! This is also setting you apart for setting standard for other's to follow and encouraging them to treat you with similar respect. This is to say, do to others, as you want them to do to you.

Your children must be taught what is called home training to respect the difference in people whether their color, race, religion or culture. People do things differently as your child have to understand from his or her own family because of race, culture or religion. So teach your children to respect other family culture, race or religion and to understanding that different family does things differently. Families like having their own traditional way of doing things that are important and very meaningful to them.

Children should be trained about good manners and true education by their parents as soon as they can understand what is right from wrong. Every child need to be taught and reminded on manner throughout their childhood and parent should give positive follow-up when your child does something right. Let your child be aware of it and when your child does something wrong also, do not be negative about it, but gently tell him or her how it is best done right and the reason so. It is your responsibility as a parent to teach and instill discipline within the heart of your child and the wisdom and knowledge of God.

The education of every human being is in true scriptural righteousness, perfecting the man of God, and enduring him with power for all good work. As a parent, you need to know that the deeds of your child makes known what he or she is made of and what your child will be if that child is not properly trained. For the Bible says, "Even a child is known by his doings, whether his work be pure, and whether it be right!" (Proverbs 20:11.)

Let me encourage every parent that dearly loves their children very much, to always remember what the scripture says about training them? "Don't fail to correct your children. They won't die if you spank them. Physical discipline may well save them from death."(Proverbs 23:13.) This is to say that you do not hesitate to correct your child, even if you have to use rod. You will not kill him or her, but you will save your child soul from hell.

A spoiled child will bring disgrace and shame to his or her mother like the bible says "To discipline and reprimand a child produces wisdom, but a mother is disgraced by an undisciplined child."(Proverbs 29:15.) I am not encouraging child abuse or say you should mistreatment your children but correct them in love.

Child abuse is not right and is not of God. I believe the reason why many children don't have the fear of God or their parent otherwise have no conscience is because they don't care to know the right from wrong and that's why it doesn't bother them to stab or kill a stranger, their friend, their school mate or even their own parents.

CHAPTER 14

Secrets of Keeping Your Fight Fair and Your Marriage Strong

In marriage, there are two emotional reality, i.e. his and hers. The root of the emotional difference is partly biological which can be traced to the different training boys and girls received about handling emotion. Boys play in larger groups and in their interactions, they learn to negotiate role and status but girls tend to play in pair or small group and put emphasis on relationship. When boys are playing and one of them gets hurt and is upset, the other boys will expect him to continue playing or get out of the way so that the game can continue.

But when the girls are playing and if one of them gets hurt, the game stops and everyone gathers around to help. This shows the fact that boys take pride in their independence while girls see themselves as part of a web of connections and they feel threatened by any rupture in the relationship. These can be interpreted as the fact that women enter into marriage well prepared for the role of emotional manager while men are not so equipped. The gender gap is critical for the married couple as concerns of handling disagreements.

The way and method of disciplining your children is not what make your marriage good or bad. Rather it is how the husband and wife relate with one another over issues that matter most. Many marriage problems starts with Contempt, disgust and personal attack and this can trigger off "flooding". A "flooded" husband or wife may be so over-whelmed by the partner's negative posture to the extent that his or her reactions may be swamped by dreadful, out of control feelings. A man or woman in this state of mind will find it difficult to organize his or her thinking and will fall back to primitive reactions like shouting or hitting his or hers spouse.

You need to realize that fighting your spouse every day is damaging to your marriage but fleeing can be more destructive, especially when the "flight" is a retreat into "stony silence". But "Stone walling" is the worst type of the destructive fight of running away from your spouse. The "stone-Waller" just goes blank and withdraws completely from conversation. In 85% of marriages, it is the husband who "stone wall" as a defensive strategy against a critical wife. I want you to understand that as a married man or woman that habitual "stone walling" is devastating and destructive to your marriage because it cuts off all possibility of working out disagreement.

Once "flooded," a man secrete more adrenalin into his blood stream than a "flooded" wife and the effect also takes longer to dissipate in men than in women. Furthermore husbands must realize that "stone walling" will make his heart beat rate to drop by about ten beats, giving him a sense of relief but the sad thing about this is that it will however shoot up the heart beat rate of your wife to the level that will signal high distress and this will not help the wellbeing of relationship.

One of the issues that are mostly common with women especially in marriage which should be avoided at all cost is the issue of making reference to the past negative experience if you want to enjoy your marriage. You should concentrate on the present issue at hand and not referring to the old issue. An old settled issue should not be dragged into the present matter or any other old grievance or history of disagreement. Most men don't like any woman referring to the past mistake and use it against them. It makes men to switch off completely and this every wife must understand if you want to enjoy your husband.

Each partner must be given the chance to express his or her point and opinion. The truth of the whole matter is to stay calm at the first sign of flooding and have a break. You should cool down by practicing a relaxation technique or aerobic exercise. You may breathe in and count up to twenty and breathe out and do likewise. May I encourage both husband and wife that no matter what the issue may be, you must not resort to name-calling? The wife should reject the temptation of calling her husband egotistical. You need to understand that a total attack on your spouse will make him or her ashamed, disliked, inadequate and on the defensive.

Let me encourage both husband and wife to understand that it is not easy to make marriage work but only by the grace of God that makes one to have a successful marriage. Every husband and wife must understand that honeymoon days of love fantasies will not last long if the creator and originator of marriage institution are pushed aside by married couples. When the "in-love" days are over and the rose tint in the eye glasses turn so crystal clear that they magnify every fault, it should not be taken that the awareness of faults, a minor diminution of first ecstasy of love, etc, is a proof that marriage is a useless exercise in failure.

To a certain extent, it is indications that the couple needs to work on accept one another in spite of fault and difference. The couple needs to turn everything over to God, the originator of marriage. It cannot be over-emphasized that God is the only one who can make marriage succeed. God's idea of marriage is a life-long institution of real and daily commitment to live and communicate love, tolerance, patience and emotional stability.

The truth is that every marriage will certainly meet challenge one time along the way. I believe God's grace will permit His children to be over-comers of marriage and life challenge. I want you to understand that husband and wife that discover each other's faults but instead of allowing the faults to destroy their marriage, but pray and stand together to face the problems will definitely win in Jesus name. Believe me, the real victory of long years of good marriage is not that the couple did not go through daily challenge like everyone else but they choose to stay together over years and face the challenge together. These make their love for one another becoming stronger than ever.

You have to understand that no one is an Ireland, so the individual member in a marriage must not see him or herself as being independent as there is no independence in marriage institution. This institution of marriage is for both husband and wife to complement one another even though they are unique individuals. There are things in this life that a man can do better that a woman cannot and vice versa. God made things that way and everyone must accept it like that. Remember in the beginning when Eve decided to act independently without Adam, the result is here for everyone to see till today that things got out of hands and man fell. Marriage is the working together of two people, (husband and wife) so that there may be all round blessing.

Let me encourage every husband and wife not to fall for the lie of the devil that says even married people should hold on to their independence.

Something like (wife must not submit to her husband) or (remain single) etc, contrary to what the Bible says that, "Wives, submit to your husband's as to the Lord. For the husband is the head of the wife as Christ is the head of the Church". (Ephesians 5:22-23.) Every marriage should be of God, the unseen member of your home if you allow him. (Ephesians 5:25) says that husband must love his wife just as Christ loves the Church and gave himself up for her. He, who loves his wife, loves himself similarly she who love her husband loves herself.

I believe when you give everything to Jesus in your marriage, He will bring you and your spouse together with his authority and grace. God's intention for marriage is to be stable, rewarding and fulfilling. You should repent if you have rebelled against God in any area concerning this. Husband and wife should submit to God and to one another. Commitment to God and to your marriage vow should make your marital relationship grow every day to have a good marriage.

Nowadays many married couples that have married for quite a while complained that their partner have changed to somebody else they don't understand anymore. The truth is that many couples did not consult the originator of marriage before they started their relationship in the first instance. If you want your husband or wife to change for the best, you yourself should take steps for positive change. There are many things in life that only prayers, fasting and the help of the Holy Spirit can change and marriage is one of them.

Take the step daily to pray for change by the power of the Holy Spirit for a better relationship, love, and wisdom and God grace to remove anything that Satan may be using to attack your marriage. Seek God face for the love of Christ and the peace of God that surpasses all human understanding with patience to deal with every situation in your marriage. Always remember that there is nothing impossible for God to handle including your marital challenges.

Some times, married couples play the blaming game which is not helpful to the goodness of their marriage. It is not a good sight for husband to bully his wife or the wife to bully her husband. Any husband or wife doing this should stop this evil habit because it is not of God. This type of atmosphere is not conducive to bring up godly children. This kind of bad habit may lead especially the husband into wife beater and that experience in the family may make the female child to be afraid to get into marital relationship. Similarly the male child may turn out later in life to be wife-beater as his father.

Let me encourage both husband and wife to always complement one another because this goes a long way. One thing I want you to understand is that if you are perfect, you will not need anyone to complement you but the truth is that no one is perfect. This I will say to every wife to give respect to her husband as he is God's chosen head of your home. Similarly every husband must love his wife as Christ love the church that He gave his life for them.

Let every real man remind himself that he is the husband and the head of his home and that he loves his wife no matter what. A real man will always appreciate his wife and express it more often and model her to their children to see. As a real man, you should not humiliate your wife in anyway, or attack people that are dear to her.

It is better for couples to engage in a non-violent verbal fight where you can express whatever bothers you than to keep icy silence. Husband and wife have to think and practice daily how they can make one another happy and not miserable. You should know that silence is a form of emotional torture and husband and wife must not engage in this type of bad habit. It is bad enough that husband and wife punish one another by cutting off and refusing to acknowledge each other's presence. A real man must accept that love is a very delicate feeling and it does not thrive in an environment that is not pleasant or that is full of anger, blame or hatred. Love grows and does well only in an atmosphere of acceptance, respect and honesty.

Every husband that is a real man must try and do his best to appreciate his wife by acknowledge and be kind to her always. This is another way to overcome selfishness but you have to understand the three negative attitudes that you have to eliminate before you can reach the stage to overcome selfishness completely. They are:

(a) Unrealistic expectations.
(b) Conscious amnesia and the sense of entitlement.
(c) I know that a sense of entitlement or expectation leads to a state of conscious amnesia. As a sense of entitlement which means whatever you does for me, I deserve it, so why should I bother to thank you.

I believe that the real man must always be polite, kind and considerate to his wife. The real man will regularly remember that he should never do to his wife what he will not want her to do to him. You should not assume that you know what your wife is thinking and how she feels all the time. You need to understand that you may be wrong now and again, and that may cause unnecessary conflict in your home. So, every husband must always encourage his wife to express herself in a manner that will not lead to emotional disagreement in the home.

Let me ask how you will feel if your wife has to interpret every look or body language you make. So in order to avoid misinterpret your wife every move, you have to to be clear regarding the perception of her. You need to be attentive to what your wife say in an open and loving approach but I can understand that this is a problem to most men. That is why I'm suggesting to every husband to practice active listening skill by non-verbal approach. This demonstrating that you are paying attention to what your wife says. You should maintain eye contact and maybe hold her hands or embrace her in a caring mode.

Many couple is often afraid to say no to his or her spouse just to avoid the partner getting upset. Most times the disagreeing partner may be scared to say: "I'm sorry, I just don't want to do that," because his or her partner may be disappointed and the disagreeing one may feel guilty. A lot of people instead of asserting themselves and saying what they want, end up doing the opposite and feel angry and awful at the end.

I recognize that there is a problem with saying yes when you mean no as this makes you not to be real in your relationship. I can understand sometimes you may do that to avoid argument or cause embarrassment to your spouse but it is nice to express true feelings and desires to your spouse as this will enable you to relate to the real person and not the fictitious one. It has been proven that assumption, illusion and fantasies are exposed as false or partially true.

May I encourage you as a real man not play the blame game in your marriage? Such as, "It's your fault, you made me do it", or "You are the reason I feel unhappy everyday". As a husband you need to always restrain yourself not to react to your wife comments and reaction when she is angry with you or when there is a problem in your home. Then you should ask yourself! "What is your part in creating this problem between you and your wife?"

I want you to understand that blame is a form of disempowerment and when you blame your spouse, what you are saying is that it is your spouse that controls your way of thinking and behaviour. The blame game denies your spouse the opportunities of deep thought about your words and rob your spouse response in a considerate manner. This is to say that instead of expressing your real grievance and feelings, you accuse and make threats.

The truth about blame is that it is a negative response to take responsibility. I understand that to take responsibility may be difficult at first but by endeavor and practice, you may get rid of the feeling of being right before you know it which is really what is behind the blame game.

I pray that as you read this book, the eyes of the understanding of your marriage be open by the fire of the Holy Spirit in Jesus name. You must not believe the lies that Satan tell you and play on your emotion by creating an opportunity for argument and strife to destroy your marriage. Satan is using the deception of disagreement and misunderstanding between you and your spouse and you always fall for it.

It brings you worrying, anxiety, short of joy, and disturbing you from focal point of what God desire to do within your family. Satan is a liar, you just have to step back, keep quiet when you are angry not to say or do anything you will regret later. Marriage, a miracle of completion book is an eye opener that will help you to learn, practice and pray your ways to a successful marital life.

CHAPTER 15

Avoid Destructive Temptation

Marriage is exceptionally beneficial to society because it is the foundation of the family and the fundamental building block of society.

- It bring significant stability and meaning to human relationships.
- It remains the ideal to raise children.
- It plays an important role in transmitting culture and civilization to future generations.

I believe that marriage is not merely a private contract, but a social institution of great public value and concern. As social science research and government surveys increasingly show, the decline in marriage since the 1960s has been accompanied by a rise in a number of serious social problems. Marriage has been spiritually, morally and traditionally understood as the union between one man and one woman.

Marriage is valuable and is worth every experience and blessing that go with it. As this generation becomes more dissolute and enlighten, the value of relationship and the integrity of marriage go downhill. The present society is regularly hyped by the media to live together without getting married; and it is so disappointing even the government of the day is encouraging cohabit between a man and a woman that are not married to each other.

Let me encourage you to avoid the lies that the devil is telling people that is seeing intimacy as cheap, simple and humiliating. I believe you need to create a protective fence to avoid the lies of the devil so that you don't be one of his victims. For example, if you are on a diet to lose weight, you have to stay away from places that serve fattening foods and likewise if you want to keep your eyes and mind where they belong, you must avoid going to places where you will come across enticement. You have to focus on where you are going and have a discipline of being in control. You have to keep your mind occupied with things that interest you that is godly, so that you can avoid temptation.

The Bible views physical approach of the relationship between husband and wife as the earnest form of bond. It is the most cherished well-expressed extension of love; deepen of giving pleasure of building and strengthening a marriage. It is a means of procreation instituted by God. I believe sex in marriage is incredibly powerful, but must be merged with holiness to give it meaning. The power of sex in marriage according to the scriptures when used right helps couples to grow in love. It enhances their sense of self and brings a spirit of holiness to their home.

You need to understand that these same acts of sex can also be harmful if use in the negative approach. It can water down the power of intimacy, lower the individuals and bring an inner sense of shame. This kind of talk will not be understood by an eight year old child but children need to be told about the incredible wisdom of God when they are old enough to understand. Children can be introduced to the idea that pleasure is a gift which should be used at the right time and under the right circumstances when the gift can have the most meaningful result.

The fifth of the Ten Commandments says: "Honour your parents". I believe you want your children to treat you with respect not because you are motivated by your own egos or drive for power or control but because it is good for your child and for his or her character development. The truth is that polite children are much more pleasant to live with. Your children should appreciate you even if you may have not done the best job of parenthood. But teaching them to honour you as their mother or father help them to see more clearly the debt of gratitude owed to God for everything. Every parent must teach the children in their care to respect the authorities God place on them in social, legal and spiritual level.

These days, most women focus more on their careers at the expense of their cherished relationship with their husband and these has damage many homes that the husband have to move out of the family home. This is not the will of God for Christian homes. The truth is that Satan just wants to destroy the importance of marriage so that the children of such homes may face untold misery. The situation will be that what both parents is suppose to do will be done by only one person either the mother most of the time or the father which rarely happened.

In this modern time, most women that send their husband out of their family home that they later realize their mistakes, blame mid-life crisis. They send their husband off into the arms of another woman that knows the importance of a man at home. These women accept as true the lies of the feminist movement that says women should put themselves and their careers first and treat their husband with extreme disregard. These lies are planted in the women liberation movement mentality by Satan and this mindset has robbed majority of them the joy and the happiness of having a good matrimonial home.

Many women when they are young have the dream of getting married one day and having a happy home with peace of mind. They really prepared from the beginning to fulfill the desires of their husband and put their husband desires above their own. But after the wedding ceremony, things start to change from what they dream of marriage to be into something they did not envisage within the short period of their marriage. Let me encourage you so that you can understand that the first two to ten year of any marriage is really a testing time for the marriage to succeed.

Therefore, hold tight to your marriage so that no matter what the storm may be, you must believe what the Bible says about your marriage, nevertheless what the situation may looks like. You have to let your husband be the leader of your home and give him every support and respect he deserved. The scripture says that the woman is the help meet of her husband and not head mate.

Hear what the Bible says that "To the woman he said, I will make your pains in childbearing very severe; with painful labour you will give birth to children. Your desire will be for your husband, and he will rule over you." (Genesis 3:16.) Apart from obey and comply with this instruction from God, it means you are fighting against the Word of God.

At this moment, I want every husband to understand that God will judge him for his family and I know that it is not too late for you to restore back every blessing that your family deserve. Pay attention to what the Bible says that God did not ask Eve first but Adam, (Genesis 3:9.) Additionally the Bible says that God cursed Adam because he listened to the voice of Eve (his wife) and disobeyed God. (Genesis 3:17.)

I want every married woman to comprehend that being married is a ministry in itself, to support your husband to be fulfilled in every area of his life. This I believe that the joy of every parents is to see their children successful in life. Furthermore, I know that nothing makes a woman more fulfilled than being a mother looking after her children and this is one of the happiest times in every woman's life.

You need to understand that at any time in marriage that the wife is trying to take control or be in charge of the home while the husband is still alive, there will always be tension everywhere. However, if the wife is submissive to her husband in reverence, kind and courteous, her husband will become more loving and ready to go all the way so that his wife is happy and protected. This is the secret that never fails that every wife that wants to have a good marital life must hold on to, so that she can have peace and joy in her matrimonial home.

Every wife that wants to become (Proverbs 31:10-31) woman have to understand that God wired a woman to help her husband to achieve his destiny on earth so that she as a wife of good character may be fulfilled, blessed and accomplishes everything she do. Every wife have to understand that too much nagging, bullying and criticizing her husband will make him less productive and less sure of himself. Married women should give regard to her husbands' feelings, needs and desires and absolutely he too will go all the way to make sure that his home is peaceful.

Let me encourage every married woman that wants to have a strong marital relationship must stop proving equality with her husband. It cannot work and it will not work to have two drivers driving one vehicle at the same time. Certainly the vehicle will end up in the ditch and that is tragedy. I believe a woman is created by God to help her husband to accomplish his destiny and not for you as the wife to mess up his destiny. Every Woman has to come to the understanding that God wired a man differently from a Woman. If God wants you as the wife to lead your home, He will have created you as the man.

God created the male (the husband) as the donor in terms of sexual contact while the woman is the recipient for pleasure and to have children. A man's physical and mental structure is completely different from that of a woman. These differences enrich the marital relationship and provide balance in the home. Majority of married men love to provide and protect his family unit but will go crazy when his wife rob him of his sense of worth.

It is devastating for a man when this happens and he cannot comprehend it for his wife to treat him poorly. It is true that married women like bonding with other women and loving but please do not insist that your husband's must be the same. You need to accept your husband as the head of the home, value him and encourage him to be God-fearing.

Further more, don't try to change your husband to the way you want him to be but change your own attitude to him first then you will see that he will change for the best. As a married woman, be pleasing to your husband by looking attractive for him to your best in all manners of living. Let me encourage you today to start and see your husband as a gift from God by treating him well as a service to God. The scriptures say that a good wife is from the Lord and this is why every wife must find joy, happiness and fulfillment in their marriage.

Let me challenge every good wife to try everything possible to love and nurture your husband more and more every day as a service to God other than focus only on your own career needs and aspiration of life. There is something that seems to escape the mind of many people that men and women are not created in the same way so they can not think and act the same way. Many women expect their husband to sit around and talk about his feelings to them but unfortunately men are not created to do much talking. These days, women think that giving birth and caring for a baby is a form of oppression but they have forgotten that it is a form of rewarding that every woman can experience.

I want every good wife to understand and grasp this truth that the day your desire shift away from your husband to your children or to anyone else is the day you have lost him and you are in disobedience to God. Let look at it this way, everything is centered to your children nowadays. You have forgotten that your husband that was there before the children and your mentality nowadays that he does not know how to do anything right anymore is still going to be there when your children leaves home one day.

Then how are you going to cope when the children have left home because your husband will have being a total stranger to you. The truth is that you have been using the children to fill the gap you have created against him. These is one of the reason why we have many marriages especially (Christian marriages) that have been doing well when the children are still at home but broken down when the children are no longer at home. Think about it, why a marriage couple of twenty or thirty years all of a sudden getting divorce.

May I suggest that you take my advice so that you don't make the same mistake of the people before you? You have endured for so long in your marriage with your husband and all of a sudden you are going through divorce or separation because you have used the love and affection that is due to husband for your children. This is one of the reasons nowadays that a number of Christian marriages are struggling or going through separation now.

Now is the time you need to realize such mistake and rectify it before it is too late. Remember that your children will leave home one day and it will remain you and your husband alone at home. You better start loving your husband as it is from the beginning of your marriage so that you don't fill empty and lonely in the end. You may not believe and accept it, but it is the truth. The truth is that many husbands have been emotionally abused and castrated by his wife by experience regular and daily harassment. It is hard for any man under that situation to be productive in life.

It is as bad as a wife can hardly talk to her husband without frequently criticizing him. What really amazes me is these so called civilize culture or career women mentality that always devotes a hundred times more energy to pleasing and respecting their managers at work place or the pastor at their church than she does pleasing her husband at home. The attitudes of such women have destroyed many homes, and their children have been badly affected because of this. There is a saying that if you treat your husband like an expert I tell you, he will become one before you know it. Let me encourage to express gratitude even for the smallest things that your husband do for you and I want you to understand that men get distracted easily even though it should not be like that but never criticize them, simply remind them gently of their goals.

These days' career and fashion for women is having priority over pleasing the husband. The present day wife is totally different from the good married women of old. In the early sixties and seventies, married women in their late 30s made love on average more than twice in a week because keeping her husband happy is her priority along with cooking, cleaning and caring for her children. But nowadays, a wife only has time to make love once in a week or not at all. The problem is that at the end of the day modern wife are less active at home and don't longer feels obliged to fulfill their wifely duties to their husband. The older women of old devoted their time to look after their family and particularly the needs of their husband. This is why there were fewer divorce rates then than what we have these days.

You need to understand my point here that I'm not discredit the modern day wife but to encourage them to put a sense of balance on whatever decision they are going to make concerning their home. I do understand that many women have to fit in career, relationship, and children and home together. I thank God for every wife having all that accomplishment but you don't have to neglect your husband sexual need because of your career or aspiration. Let me encourage you use your husband sexual need as your own way of relaxing and enjoying your marriage to the full by using it to remove all the stress of the day out of your system.

In this day and age, what majorities of husband want are respect, appreciation and love from his wife. I want every wife to know that the compliment you give to your husband go a long way in uplifting him. The opinion any wife has of her husband is very vital and important because a lot of wife do not understand her husband as far as opinions is concerned. One of the things a good wife has to know and understand about her husband is that you give your suggestion, while your husband may not say whether he accepts it or not. You must understand that your husband has taking it on board, and it is up to him to act immediately or not. The problem with many wives is that they want to force their husband to act immediately. Remember your husband is not your child and he is not a dog that you command.

This is the wisdom that every wife needs to know and adhere to in order to enjoy a peaceful home. I believe good attitude goes a long way and if you as the wife treasure your husband and appreciate him as the king in your home, he will treat you like a queen. Husband and wife need to appreciate one another, for example, when the husband stays at home for the day to look after the children, and the wife comes home. She should be grateful like saying, "thanks for preparing dinner tonight". The wife must not take her husband for granted that this is part of his responsibility anyway! An appreciative wife is always focusing on the tasks done and not on the long list of unaccomplished chores left undone.

Many wives put their frustrations to be their husbands' fault. The reason is that they don't understand themselves, not to talk about understanding their husband. Let me encourage you, if you are in the category of a wife that doesn't understand herself. What you need to do is to start to believe the Word of God for your life and your marriage. Before long, you will start to understand yourself and your husband than ever before through the Word of God. What I want you to understand is that any wife that doesn't appreciate her husband and drove him out of their matrimonial home, the truth is, another woman will appreciate him and take care of him.

Appreciate your husband means giving him the focus of your undivided attention at some point in time even if it is only ten to twenty minutes daily. You as a wife should let her husband know all the time that you are proud of him like saying, "you handle the other driver courteously, well done." By this type of statement any man will always feel responsible and appreciated and he will be proud of you too. You see, I'm only encouraging you to do what you are suppose to do as a married woman to encourage your husband and be fulfilled most of the time. I want both husband and wife to know and understand that marriage is not about give and take; marriage is not fifty-fifty; marriage is not about equal division of labor but it is about each side giving and continuing to give one hundred percent all the time.

Many men have forgotten that they are the husband due to the circumstance or situation that surrounds them. May I encourage every husband to remind himself of this fact as the head of his home and to love his wife as a service to God daily in every situation with patience and forgiveness? Be a Godly husband and be kind to your wife, appreciate her for who she is and do this to the awareness of your children. It is not a good practice for any husband or wife to belittle his or her spouse in the presence of their children because it will bring indiscipline's problems in their home.

I believe one of the secrets for long lasting and strong marital life is for both husband and wife to have the attitude of given gift to one another. The more you give to your spouse, the more your love will grow. It is a good habit for husband and wife to pray for one another for wisdom, patience endurance to grow in love daily. What I want you to understand is that it takes a lot of work to create a lasting and loving marital life. Marriage demands a lot from both husband and wife in everything concerning their relationship. There is no other relationship that has the potential to create such a deep bond that offers such an opportunity for personal and spiritual growth. The test for true soul mates is to learn how to create the love that succeeds in breaking down the barrier of ego, and selfishness that enabling one another to reach genuine intimacy.

I know that several people don't understand what it actually means to love someone. These days most love is base on material things and possessions of either the man or the woman. For instance, "people always say that they fall in love". Fall means to stumble or trip and be out of control. Do you mean that love is an accident? An unconscious descent into the unknown! Is love something that bypasses conscious choice and rationality? Some people say: "I'm crazy about you", "She's mad about him", "I can't live without you". One would think from all this that love is a temporary state of insanity, illusion, a psychotic affair. This type of obsessive love belief may serve as a temporary antidote to loneliness, depression and insecurity, but it is not true love.

Nobody falls in love because love must be created. You must act lovingly by giving to your partner and as a function of giving, you create love. You have to understand that the more of yourself you invest in anything or anybody, the more attached you feel to that person or item. A house you build with your hands is a house that you will love. To have genuine love is for you not to think of what your partner can do for you but what you can do for your partner. I pray for you to develop true love with wisdom, patience and endurance so that your marriage can be a miracle of completion in Jesus name. Amen.

CHAPTER 16

Marriage and Money

One of the crucial things you have to understand in marriage as husband and wife is to know that money is not an end but a means to an end. The heartbreak nowadays is that 65% of marriage divorces are directly related to financial issues and more indirectly related. Many husband and wife have fallen into the trap of covetousness and riches that destroy their marriage. The truth I want you to know and follow is that Godliness with sufficient material blessings of food and clothing should make you and I content with life but many husband and wife have ignored these principles. These have affected many families today going through divorce and their children suffer the emotional stress for the mistake of their parent.

Apostle Paul wrote to Timothy that "Yet true religion with contentment is great wealth. After all, we didn't bring anything with us when we came into the world, and we certainly cannot carry anything with us when we die. So if we have enough food and clothing, let us be content. But people who long to be rich fall into temptation and are trapped by many foolish and harmful desires that plunge them into ruin and destruction. For the love of money is at the root of all kinds of evil. And some people, craving money, have wandered from the faith and pierced themselves with many sorrows." (1 Timothy 6:6-10.) I believe that not money itself is evil but the love of it.

We all need money could use a little more right now. Many people do not want to talk about it especially husband and wife. Loads of money or in particular lack of it can be a major source of marital problems. Many people will assume or think that if they are rich, all their problems will vanish but this reality is more difficult to swallow. One thing we should all understand is that there are particular struggles in being poor as well as a distinctive challenge in being wealthy. In view of the fact that we all need money and having it is not the problem, then what is the "love of money" then? In my opinion, the love of money is when you will do anything for the sake of money such as desert your family in search of money. People that kill another for the sake of making more money have the love of money in their heart. People that steal from the government coffer to satisfy their greed and selfishness have the love of money in their heart.

You need to understand that your attitude as a parent towards money is likely to shape your children attitude toward money too. You have to realize that the past shapes the present and your attitude towards money and the importance you put on it from your childhood will affect your attitude towards money in your marriage. You need to understand that money is essentially neutral, but it can mean so much. Money can be a source of security or anxiety in the home and can be an opportunity or reminder of importance. We can use money as a family to improve our lives or use it to destroy our destiny. Money in the family can lead us into financial freedom or serve as a yoke around our neck.

As a parent, you have to understand that just as the attitude of your parents that affects you so is your attitude to money will also have an impact on your children. Before it's too late, you have to recognize and eradicate any negative attitude you have toward money so that you don't pass it down to your children. You should take a few seconds and examine your attitude towards money that you unconsciously impact on your children. Think about your earliest memory concerning money i.e. that car or cloth you wanted but never got.

Think how you feel when you have enough money in your pocket compared to when you have little or nothing. How is the mood in your home when there is a financial challenge? I believe the answer to this question will not change the balance in your bank account but it may provide you with a deeper understanding of money that could ease the tension surrounding your home and marriage.

You have to understand that the ultimate goal of money and marriage is for husband and wife to have the same vision as one. Husband and wife need to plan their resources together by budgeting as one and they should have the same value of life. Three times the Bible says in (Genesis 2:24, Matthew 19:5 and Ephesians 5:31), "and two shall become one". This indicates that becoming one is an important ingredient in the success of any marriage. The truth is that becoming one comes in many ways such as praying together as much as you can in one spirit. Knowing what your partner will say or do even when you may not have discussed it together before is an indication of knowing one another reasonably well and being in oneness.

A further mode of becoming in oneness is by sexual bond between husband and wife so that unfaithfulness will have no chance in the marriage. However one area that is very crucial in marriage that is a problem to many is the area of money which is very important in our lives. I can understand that becoming in oneness financially is very difficult in certain part of the world due to their culture and their way of thinking. The husband would not want his wife to know how much he earns. He will be hiding money from his wife and likewise the wife will always be saying there is no money, however there is money she is hiding somewhere in the house.

I want you to understand the importance of becoming oneness in marriage by having a joint account so that not only are you connected physically but in monetary matter as well. This encourages trust between husband and wife with time and it helps with future planning as it is the "perfect will" of God for us to be one. That is why I want you to understand why rich people are not happy nowadays likewise the poor people are not happy too due to their misunderstanding of wealth. The truth is that there is no real connection between wealth and true happiness. Then you can ask yourself. What is true happiness?

Well, well, well, let me say to you that for every human being, true happiness is a state of integrity, where all the parts of you fit together to form a whole and you have no internal conflict. You are not lying, cheating or stealing. You are not doing something you don't want to do, or holding back from doing something you do want to do. If you are in a state of integrity, you will feel joy, and this is what people commonly mean by true happiness. I can say positively that true happiness is one the most important thing everybody seeks for in life. But despite what you read and hear, true happiness can't be bought or created as such. You have to cultivate it; in short, you have to discover how to be happy from within yourself.

I believe that your quest for true happiness starts from home with yourself, your spouse and your children. It's all about having self-esteem and valuing yourself instead of putting yourself down. Having confidence in yourself doesn't make you into some sort of horrible person that you have to apologize for everything. Consequently it means you're responsible and you're proud of what you have achieved so far and as a replacement for the challenges you have face before, you decide to focus on the positive. True happiness comes to anyone who takes joy in his or her lot.

Let me encourage you as husband and wife to be more affectionate and endure in everything especially money matters for your home. So that you focus less on things that dissatisfied you in the past and be free from stressful thoughts about the future. You need to put your center of attention on the present kindness of God every day as husband and wife. As you do this, your mind will not wander unnecessarily to some thoughts that are not conducive to the appreciation of the kindness of God.

God will gently move your awareness to the ever constant presence of His kindness that you have to experience. I want you to grow and be conscious so that your mind will have the ability to direct your thought to the kindness of God. As you start a new journey of happiness and accomplishment in your marital life, you will realize more of the kindness of God more than ever before. This will make you aware that Marriage is a miracle of completion.

CHAPTER 17

Marriage is a Blessing and a Privilege From God

Marriage is the great institution that God designed and must be support, recognize, commemorate and be esteem as God holy matrimony. Being a married man or woman is a privilege that should be treasured. Many people have not realized the significance of marriage, moreover that is why they abuse, assault and drag theirs in the mud until it is too late to put right.

Let every person reading this book know that God's kindness is upon any one who carry out His original creative purpose to multiply and replenish the earth. That is why every husband and wife must realize that any unsupportive decision you make concerning your marriage will not only have an effect on you and your spouse but have effect on subsequently generation to come.

The Bible says that, "Give honour to marriage, and remain faithful to one another in marriage. God will surely judge people who are immoral and those who commit adultery." (Hebrew 13:4.) So every husband and wife must think correctly if need be, seek for marriage counseling if you are experiencing challenges in your marriage. Every married man or woman has to understand that your spouse is part of your blessing and your destiny on this earth.

You have to value, respect and celebrate one another as long as both of you shall live. You need to thank God for what you have and continue to believe Him for what you don't have. You know what, somebody somewhere is still fasting and praying for such blessing you have now that you don't appreciate. Listen to me, someone wants to be like you although you may not believe this but it is true.

Let me share this secret with you as your daily obligation. While you wake up next to your spouse in the morning, look your spouse in the eyes and say "Thank you Father God for another beautiful and blessing day". The truth is that God kept His angels around you and your family every moment of the night. You did not wake up in the hospital with tubes running from your nose; hello, that's a blessing. Many people never made it through the night but you, your spouse and your children do. You have to make it a habit to thank God for His goodness every morning.

Truth be told, lots of men and women have never been married once in their life but you do. Every husband must thank God for his wife and children daily, likewise every wife must thank God for her husband and children daily. Do you realize the gladness of seeing your children come running out to greet you when you come back home and you open your arms out to welcome them?

You see, that's a joy and a blessing. Please, don't get me wrong here. Many still believe God for a child. Their house is silent with the echoes of loneliness. But your children are around you, so you have to remember at all times that this in itself is a blessing. The Bible says that, "Happy, blessed, and fortunate is the man whose quiver is filled with them! They will not be put to shame when they speak with their adversaries at the city gate" (Psalm 127:5.) Thank God for everything because He loves you with an everlasting love.

Encouragement for Healthy Marital Lifestyle!

You need to spend quality time together regularly with your spouse even in a tight schedule for heart to heart talk. The type of communication that will stand the test of time in love and truth during marital challenge that will draw both of you closer. Both husband and wife must put into practice forgiveness when you are upset by your spouse. I want you to know that forgiveness are vital for a successful marriage and sometimes it is a process and it take time.

Forgiveness is letting go of the need for revenge and releasing negative thoughts of bitterness and offense. Husband and wife can provide a wonderful model for their children by forgiving. Fathers must know that if your children observe your reconciliation with their mum or their mum reconcile with their dad, who is at the wrong, perhaps they may learn not to harbour bitterness over the ways in which you may have disappointed them.

To everyone that is not yet marries, forgiveness is still an extremely valuable skill to have for a good life. Everyone need forgiveness especially husband and wife to have fun together, because couple that has fun together stay together. Be spur-of-the-moment even in any little time you may share together because it will have a big result on your marital life. So make time to spend quality time together.

Additional, I want you to know that kindness is a good habit to practice as married couple because it is a spontaneous gesture of goodwill towards one another. Kind words and deeds come from a state of benevolence generated by a core response deep within all of us. When husband and wife carry out an act of kindness, it is a message from one heart to another. That is an act of love, an unspoken "I care" statement. May I encourage every husband and wife to continue performing an act of kindheartedness each day to one another such as smiling and greeting your spouse in a delightful mode?

Compliment your spouse regarding his or her hair, eyes, smile, and laugh or an item of clothing. It is an excellent gesture to affirm your spouse caring attitude and something he or she accomplish or have completed well. Even small things like helping your spouse put on or off his or her coat, opening the door, saying please, thank you, excuse me, and other common courtesies that unfortunately are not very common nowadays.

It may be giving your total attention to your spouse when he or she is talking. To have a long lasting and enjoyable marital life, you have to be kind, warm-hearted, sympathetic and forgiving one another. It is best at times to put your concern on hold and think about how you can show kindness to one another.

I am here to tell you that there are many ways of which you may possibly help your marriage, such as humour and laughter or a good smile whenever you are around your spouse. Laughter as someone says is the best medicine for mind and body. So, Husband and wife should laugh together more often because it improves the flow of oxygen to the heart and releases chemical in the brain which can enhance your day and reduce stress. Laughter reduces pain and allows you to tolerate discomfort. It reduces blood sugar levels, and increases glucose tolerance in diabetics and non-diabetics alike.

Laughter's role in intimate relationship is vastly underestimated, but I want you to have the understanding that it is the glue of good marital lifestyle. So, practice it daily. You need to complement one another frequently and enjoy each other differences too. The truth is, if both of you are too much alike, one of you is not needed. So, celebrate your differences and understand that the two of you together bring a combined energy and strength to the good health of your relationship.

That is why I want you to understand that intimacy is very important in marriage so that husband and wife are intimately attached. Intimacy is the tool to a healthy married life that every couple should build every day. Intimacy is "in-to-me-you-see" that means you can be who you say you really are with your spouse without the fear of rejection. You let down the guard and remove the mask and be the real you.

Enjoy the love with the closeness that is between both of you without any fear. Let it be that the more you stay together, the more your love for one another become stronger and better. It does not matter how many children you have, but the bottom line is that you have each other and you are going to enjoy each other till death do you part.

Let me remind you today that your spouse is your ministry and part of your destiny. You may not believe it but it is true. Every husband must come to term that his wife is his help meet and his ministry. When you think about love itself, you have to think about loving your spouse more. This is because your spouse is your spiritual song in the night. You spouse is your do you right. The truth I want you to know is that when a man loves himself, he loves his wife. Likewise when a man beat himself, he beats his wife. Truth be told, when a man cherishes his wife, it reinforces her value to be the best that God want her to be.

May I encourage every husband and wife not to live in bitterness or anger and in any negative mindset? The most excellent thing you can do is to enjoy the grace of God with your spouse. When there is a problem or a challenge in your marriage, the best you can do is to deal with it. Do not push disagreement under the carpet but deal with the situation once and for all.

In the same way do not avoid it because it is one of the causes for divorce rate to be high in this modern day marriages. You should avoid bottling things in because it will eventually spill out like a volcano. You need to find a way in dealing with disagreement instead of avoiding it. Even if you have to seek counseling to strengthening your marriage, it is well worth it.

Husband and wife need to make use of their difficult time to their advantage in order to move closer to each other for their relationship to become stronger. It is a good habit to develop to give gift to your spouse regularly so that you don't have to wait till the big occasion to generously show your goodness to your husband or wife.

If you are not the type that gives gifts to your spouse before, you can start to do so from now on. You can start by making your spouse a cup of tea or coffee in the morning or bringing him or her cup of water when working in the garden or busy around the house. You may start today to do at least one kindness for your spouse and I believe that your relationship will begin to stand the test of time.

I believe you want to have a good marriage and that's why you are reading this book for encouragement and inspiration so that you may have a successful marital life. You can start right away by your thought of kindness and soft tone of voice to your spouse. When you do this, it will allow your spouse to connect with you instead of pushing him or her into being defensive! Always ask the "magic" question like! "Babe" is there anything you want that I can do for you today? I know that the atmosphere will definitely change immediately. You see, that puts the drawbridge down and allow your partner to walk over to your side and let you know what she or he needs.

This is a common mistake that many husband and wife create by assuming things for their partner but got it wrong most of the time. One of the best things you can do for your marriage is to complement one another daily on something that your spouse is trying to achieve. This will always builds up confidence and brings closeness in your relationship. Always remember that it's easy to criticize, but it takes an effort and courage to give one another complement.

You can communicate effectively by sitting together facing each other to share your thought and feelings. It is a good response that you let your spouse know that you heard what he or she said, furthermore you should keep commitment as very important in your relationship to pursue whatever you say you are going to do and do it.

The truth is that there will be point in time you will be displease or upset with your spouse, nevertheless the best thing you can do is to step back and on no account say anything you will later regret. Subsequently ask yourself why you are angry; moreover deal with the anger issue immediately. Loads of times husband as well as wife venture their hurts and fear on their partner which is so unfair on the side of the other person. May I encourage you to practice a lack of false pride which is called humility? When you are wrong, come clean of your mistake and move on.

Inquire from your spouse for advice especially on topics you are not conversant with or not sure about and don't be "a know it all". I believe that no body wants to marry to a lazybones or uncaring person and that is why you have to look good for your spouse. When you take care of yourself, you will feel better about yourself and your spouse will feel proud about you.

You need to take regular exercise and eat good food so that you can enjoy your life to the full with your spouse. You do not let anything get in the way of building the kind of loving, peaceful and romantic atmosphere in your marriage. Do not allow money or job worries and the concerns of your children to stop you from building within your marriage the joy and peace that God want you to have.

I want you to know that God did not create the marriage institution between a man and a woman as a competition. Commonly husband and wife are equal however are different as God created them male and female. May I encourage you not to expose your spouse to ridicule because at the end of it all, it will come back to have an effect on you too. When both husband and wife give and serving one another, they will not have to do mathematics in their marriage. You need to give a great deal of thought and consideration to this important guidance for your marriage.

Husbands avoid being ill-tempered all the time with your wife but love and encourage her always. Give yourself to your spouse in every way you can and make him or her life full and enjoyable. Let godly wife too makes the time and effort to be her husband's "beloved" at all times. Furthermore return his affection and encourage him in every way you can. With all of these conduct and many more, husband and wife must learn to genuinely love and cherish one another. I pray that God will help you and your spouse to be in love again and again so that your marriage may be a miracle of completion.

CHAPTER 18

Factors that Will Help
Your Marriage Succeed

FIRM FOUNDATION

You have to make the Word of God, (The Bible) as your scriptural foundation for your family to withstand the storm of life when it comes? The truth is that it will definitely come one day but the season for every marriage to go through challenge is different. Successful marriage doesn't just endure automatically any more than a house just keeps standing for many years. For every good structure that wants to withstand the storms will need a strong foundation and the same is true of a successful marriage. Successful marital lifestyle is built on a true foundation of the Word of God.

There are lots of books and magazine on marriage that don't worth reading at all. Yet a number of marriage counselors will advise troubled couple to stay together because of their children while other counselor will give advice those same couple to split up. These days, many experts have changed their view on this topic because they don't have a clue on successful marital life. I want you to know that the best advice on marital relationship that in many ways reflect the best principle found is in the Word of God, (The Bible). The scriptural principle has helped many families to find true marital success and you too can take advantage of it.

The Bible makes available the firm foundation for marital and family living lifestyle. I want you to understand that the Bible is written for the schooling of mankind in true scriptural righteousness, perfecting the man of God, and enduring him with power for all good works. The truth is that, "All Scripture is inspired by God and is useful to teach us what is true and to make us realize what is wrong in our lives. It straightens us out and teaches us to do what is right. It is God's way of preparing us in every way, fully equipped for every good thing God wants us to do." (2 Timothy 3:16-17.)

COMMITMENT

Jesus said, "Since they are no longer two but one, let no one separates them, for God has joined them together" (Matthew 19:6.) May I tell you that all successful couple sees their marriage as a permanent relationship? Any time they have any challenge they strive to solve it rather than use it as an excuse to let go of their marriage. When husband and wife have a sense of commitment, they feel secured because they know that each partner trusts that the other partner will continue to esteem their relationship. The commitment I am talking about is a guide rail that will prevent your marriage from going off course.

What I would like you to understand is that commitment matter since it is the backbone of a marriage relationship. Yet after repeated mistake, misunderstanding and anger, commitment can seem more like a trap than a trust. In effect, "till death do us part" becomes little more than nothing significant any more. Let's put it this way, when you are committed and in the midst of a dispute, do not allow your mind regretting that you married your spouse. When you are committed, you do not allow your mind to day dream about being with someone other than your spouse.

When you are committed to your spouse and there is a dispute, do not tell your spouse that you are leaving, with the intention of going to find someone who appreciates you. May I challenge you to consider one or two measures you may take to strengthen your commitment to become stronger than before? Something like, writing an occasional note to your spouse that you love him or her dearly or giving your spouse a lovely flower.

You may keep the photo of your spouse and children on display at work, in your purse, or phone your spouse each day from work just to stay in touch. You may ask for suggestion from your spouse what would be most important to him or her as the relationship is concerned.

FORGIVENESS

The Bible says, "You must make allowance for each other's faults and forgive the person who offends you. Remember the Lord forgive you, as you must forgive others." (Colossians 3:13.) This is a requirement of every Christian man and woman to forgive one another even as Christ forgives you. Every successful couple learns from the past, but they do not keep tract of old grievance and then use these to make sweeping assertion, such as "you are always late" or "you never listen". Both husband and wife think that it is okay to pass over wrongdoing, though the Bible says, "People with good sense restrain their anger; they earn esteem by overlooking wrongs" (Proverbs 19:11.) This is to say a sensible man will prolong his patience and not his anger.

I would like you to know that God is ready to forgive you however that is not always the case for human. David said, "O Lord, you are so good, so ready to forgive, so full of unfailing love for all who ask your aid." (Psalms 86:5.) Every husband and wife require to understand that old wrongs left unresolved can produce layers of resentment that accumulate to the point where forgiveness will not be easily reach. This will make you and your spouse to retreat into an emotional corner. Each one of you will not care about how the other may be feeling. This may result for both of you to be ensnared in a loveless marriage.

I want you to know that this type of situation can be changed only by the grace of God first, then by your own hard work! May I suggest that you may bring out your photograph and that of your spouse taken earlier in the good days of your marriage or during your courtship days to have good memories. Try to rekindle the warmth and the love you felt before challenge creep in and clouded your view. Many times, you need to think of the qualities that first attracted you to your spouse in the first place back then? What persona do you most esteem in your spouse then and possibly now?

You can experience the positive effect that being a forgiving person might have on your whole family. It is a good attitude to develop as husband and wife to keep past grievance out of present disagreement you may have with your spouse. Thank God for your spouse and appreciate the quality you admire in him or her. This is to every husband that wants to see his wife excel all other women in wifehood, motherhood, religion and industry. For the Bible says that, "Her children stand and bless her. Her husband praises her. There are many virtuous and capable women in the world, but you surpass them all." (Proverbs 31:28-29.)

TEAMWORK

Marriage means teamwork i.e. you as the husband is the pilot and your wife is the copilot with the same flight plan. Every successful husband and wife adheres to God's headship arrangement as outline in the scriptures that says, "You wives will submit to your husband's as you do to the Lord. For a husband is the head of his wife as Christ is the head of his body, the church; he gave his life to be her Savior. As the church submits to Christ, so you wives must submit to your husband's in everything." (Ephesians 5:22-24.) Let me say this, because a number of people may not agree with me on this that obedience to the husband in all things is based upon him loving his wife, as Christ does to the church.

All the same, both husband and wife need to see their marriage in terms of "ours" and "we" rather than "mine" and "me". When there is teamwork, both husband and wife are no longer single at heart, they are "one" flesh. Hear what the Bible says that, "At last" Adam exclaimed. "She is part of my own flesh and bone! She will be called 'woman,' because she was taken out of man. This explains why a man leaves his father and mother and is joined to his wife, and the two are united into one." (Genesis 2:23-24.)

Woman is said not to have been taken out of man's head to be lorded over by him, or from his feet to be trampled on him, but from his side to be equal with him, from under his arm to be protected by him, and from near his heart to be loved by him.

Husband and wife have to be a team, so that minor events may not quickly become major issue with each one attacking the other rather that the challenge at hand. When you and your spouse are a team, you become like a pilot and copilot with the same flight plan rather than two pilots on a collision course. When you have disagreement, you work out practical solution instead of wasting time and emotional energy, blaming and accusing one another. Always make sure that you are more team oriented with your spouse and ask for suggestions so that both of you can agree on one thing.

RIGHT PRIORITY

What I want you to realize is that in every successful marriage, husband and wife puts the other's needs ahead of self, possessions, job, friends, and even other relations. They spend more time together with their children than any other person. Both husband and wife are willing to make sacrifice for the benefit of the family. They are not selfish glorying in their own gifts and graces. But are just as interested in the blessings of their spouse and rejoice to see him or her blessed. Everyone should know that the Bible places high importance on the issues of family. Apostle Paul wrote that a person, who does not provide for his family, is worse than a person without faith.

The truth of life is that over time a person priority may change. For instance, one person may focus more on his or her career than on family. The problem is that it is easier to say that we put family first than to show it. For example, you need to give attention to your spouse or your children when they need to talk as soon as possible. When talking to other people about your activities, try to discuss things you do with your family. May I challenge every husband and wife to turn down added responsibility whether at work or elsewhere if your family needed your time?

Everyone that wants to have a successful marital life have to demonstrate that their family comes first in whatever you do in life. You need to cut back on things that may be intruding on the time that would be better spent with your spouse and children. You can share your determination with your family by showing willingness to change and I believe your spouse is more likely to follow.

RESPECT

Regarding for one another is the foundation of real love and if you have not been doing this! Start from today and show more respect, then you will see how your spouse will appreciate you more. For instance, whenever you husband comes home from work or from somewhere, try as much as possible to get off the phone when he walks in through the door. Unless the phone conversation is very important or urgent!

You need to recognize his presence in the house. Respect your husband by not putting him down in public or talking to him as if he is your servant. Treat Him the way you would like to be treated i.e. treating your spouse with the same respect you show your boss at work place. Marriage is about a man and a woman work together as one because both of you need one another.

May I let you know that the foundation for a strong marriage is the ability to show love and respect, no matter the situation around you? This is a fact that many husbands can relate with about their wife because for most wife, one piece of criticism from the husband make her feel like the rug has been pulled out from under her, like her foundation has been shaken. Every person, both troubled and successful family has disagreements. What I would like you to be aware of is that successful family discusses matters without resorting to sarcasm, insults, and other forms of offensive language.

Family member treat one another as they themselves would like to be treated because this is the golden rule against self-centeredness. Jesus said, "Do for others what you would like them to do for you. This is a summary of all that is taught in the law and the prophet" (Matthew 7:12.) You should understand that words can become weapons producing devastating effect. Just as ocean waves can erode solid rock, a pattern of hurtful speech can weaken a family.

To everyone, it is better to be alone in the world than to dwell with a contentious and angry woman and likewise the same could be said of a bitter-tongue man. But when it comes to parenting, the Bible says, "Fathers, don't aggravates your children. If you do, they will become discouraged and quit trying." (Colossians 3:21.) Every parent has to love their children and understand that if you constantly criticized them; your children may come to feel that it is impossible to please you, their parents and even give up trying.

You have to make an effort that disagreements don't usually end with one person storming out of the room. When you speak to your spouse or the children, don't resort to using offensive words, such as "stupid," "idiot," or something similar. You should not raise your children in an atmosphere in which abusive language is common. You have to show respect in your language towards people especially your spouse. For example, "I feel hurt when you . . ." Rather than "You are always . . ."

BEING REASONABLE

Every successful family unit, i.e. husband and wife make allowance for one another's mistake. They are also neither unduly rigid nor overly permissive with their children. They set a modest number of household rules. When correction is needed, they give it to the proper degree. The Bible says, "But the wisdom that comes from heaven is first of all pure. It is also peace loving, gentle at all times, and willing to yield to others. It is full of mercy and good deeds. It shows no partiality and is always sincere." (James 3:17.)

Husband and wife ought to have the divine wisdom that the Bible talks about. The wisdom that is pure, holy and clean. The wisdom that is peaceable, gentle, submissive, unpretentious and kind. The wisdom that is full of mercy, that is always forgiving and without double standards.

Successful parents are being reasonable when dealing with their children. They don't discipline them excessively or are hard to please. They grant freedoms to young people who demonstrate a sense of responsibility. They do not try to micro-manage. Someone said that trying to control every aspect of an adolescent's life, is the equivalent of performing a violent and exhausting rain dance to make it rain. There won't be any rain, but you will get worn out. You have to raise your level of being reasonable by praising your spouse and avoid criticizing him or her all the time so that your relationship can be a marriage, miracle of completion.

SUBMISSION

It is one of the principles for a long-lasting marital life and is practice by women of wisdom to her husband. Several people have misunderstood the submission that God commanded between husband and wife. That is why the marriage institution is falling at an alarming rate.

I would like every wife to understand that submitting to your husband is to allow his plan ahead or before your plan because you love him; also it is a command from God. This is one of the duty of a godly wife that the Bible commanded that, "Wives, submit yourselves to your own husbands, as to the Lord." (Ephesians 5:22.) Submission in everything as to the Lord, as long as it is not sinful and criminal.

Submission is while a wife wants to go to one direction for example shopping but the husband wants her to come with him to another place different from where she wanted to go before. She so much loves her husband and respects him that she has to give up her plan and follow her husband plan by doing his will above her will. That is submission; moreover your husband will greatly love you more and will always treat you like a queen.

It is unfortunate nowadays that many wives want to have their ways ahead of their husband but this is contrary to the authority of God. The truth is that as long as your behaviour and attitude is contrary to the command that God lay down for the marriage institution, there will always be dilemma in the marriage.

Every good wife need to understand that murmuring, bickering and confrontational against your husband will never build him. However praising him into what you want him to be will raise his confidence and encourage him to be the best. When you praise him, you are magnifying him to be what God has already called him to be. Truth be told, you never talk down your husband for him to get up, but talk him up and he will get up. This is wisdom for any married woman to practice to have a marriage, a miracle of completion.

CHAPTER 19

Reasons Why Two People
are Better Than One

(HUSBAND AND WIFE)

The reason why two people are better than one, (husband and wife) is to help one another in test, loneliness and discouragements. They have more reward for their labour. One can lift the other one up when one fall and be a balance in success. Both of them can keep warm.

They can prevail against another according to the scriptures that says, "Two people can accomplish more than twice as much as one; they get a better return for their labour. If one person falls, the other can reach out and help. But people who are alone when they fall are in real trouble. And on a cold night, two under the same blanket can gain warmth from each other. But how can one be warm alone? A person standing alone can be attached and defeated, but two can stand back to back-to-back and conquer. Three are even better, for a triple braided cord is not easily broken." (Ecclesiastes 4: 9-12.)

A further reason is to strengthening in weakness when burden. You need empathy, show mercy and love. Moreover you do not brow-beat a fallen partner, and so fulfill the law of Christ as Apostle Paul said to the church of Galatians in Asian province to, "Share each others troubles and problems, and in this way obey the law of Christ. If you think you are too important to help someone in need, you are only fooling yourself. You are really a no—body." (Galatians 6: 2-3.)

Two people are better for unity in prayer. This is to say that two people can move God to get whatever they ask and agree upon in prayer. I believe that even two people can constitute a local church with God's presence assured in Christ Jesus.

This is a clear reference to the omnipresence, omniscience and omnipotence of Christ among believers as Jesus gave us the assurance saying that, "I also tell you this: If two of you agree down here on earth concerning anything you ask, my Father in heaven will do it for you. For where two or three gather together because they are mine, I am there among them." (Matthew 18: 19-20.) This is to say that anything asked for by any two in agreement shall be done and if the two of them converse together about spiritual things, they have good knowledge and understanding.

Moreover, husband and wife have a great deal of pleasure in each other's company, and much profit in their mutual instruction, advices, and reproof; they sharpen each other's countenances, quicken and comfort each other's souls, establish one another in divine truth, and strengthen each other's hands and hearts to have a marriage a miracle of completion.

CHAPTER 20

Marriage Mentors

One of the reasons why marriage is falling to a disturbing rate in particular among churchgoers is because of disobedient and misunderstanding of the Word of God concerning marriage. Furthermore, there are a small number of true marriage mentor available as well as the so called marriage counselors that are accessible these days. The truth is that there are many marriage counselors that have no good marriage experience themselves because of their lack of marriage understanding that God ordained.

May I encourage you to choose an experience and proven marriage mentor that are husband and wife if you have not got one. The husband and wife who has been there before you in relationship pursuit that have developed the right attitude that gives them confidence to take calculated risk!

The mentor that is a reservoir of marital understanding with full experience through the wisdom of God with patience that you may have a fulfilled marriage and understand the value God placed on marital relationship. You need to choose a marriage mentor that you are comfortable with; the one to open up to; that are reasonably happy and more experienced.

The couple that is obvious to purposefully invest in another couple that will effectively navigate you through the journey they have already accomplished. A married couple that will willingly shares what they know and achieved in a noncompetitive manner that represent skills, knowledge, virtue and accomplishment.

You need the mentor that will take a personal and health-felt interest in you and your spouse for development and wellbeing. The mentors that will offer support, patience and zeal while guiding you and your spouse to a new level of proficiency in your marital life especially in other areas concerning your home. The mentor that will point you to the right way that represents tangible evidence of what you and your spouse can become. The mentor that will expose your weakness to you, then take you as the recipient of their mentoring to new dreams, perspective and routine. The marriage mentoring relationship may be either long or short.

Let me encourage married couple not to wait till their marriage get into challenge situation before choosing a marriage mentor. Also when you are choosing your marriage mentor, ask God to help you choose the right couple as your marriage mentor. The marriage mentor that have the fear of God in them with supplementary know-how in terms of knowledge, yet view themselves as equal to those they mentor. The purpose of marriage mentoring is to lovingly invest in the preparation, maximization or restoration of lifelong marriage by walking alongside couple who are less experience than their mentor.

What I would like you to understand is that marital relationship takes purpose and unrelenting efforts. That is why you need marriage mentoring which will bring value, community rather than isolation into your relationship. Marriage mentoring will help married couple to have a realistic expectations especially giving them guidance since the early years of marriage are tough. Marriage mentoring will help married couples restore their marriage before it is too late by encouragement with wisdom in different stages of their marriage. Marriage mentors serves as role models with excellent resources and tools to those they are mentoring.

Let me suggest to those that wants to get marry and have a successful marital life not have anything to do with anyone that doesn't have the fear of God in them as relationship is concerned. Particularly if there is nobody he or she listens for advice concerning personal development. Truth be told, I believe there may be problem ahead if you do not take to this counsel. This is one of the reasons you have to choose an experienced and godly marriage mentor so that you may learn from their mistakes and their experience.

The Bible says, "Dear brothers and sisters honour those who are your leaders in the Lords work. They work hard among you and warn you against all that is wrong. Think highly of them and give them your wholehearted love because of their work and remember to live peaceable with each other." (1 Thessalonians 5:11-12.)

The reason why marriage mentor are different apart from marriage counselor is that marriage mentor impart knowledge and experience while marriage counselor are qualified professional that gives advice or guidance on marriages which may or may not help the marriage. Both marriage mentors and marriage counselors are important for the sustainability of marriages except that marriage mentor will walks along with you all the way from where you are to the place of success and confidence. That is why the Bible says, "And without question, the person who has the power to bless is always greater than the person who is blessed". (Hebrews 7:7.)

I believe everybody needs the Bible as their living paradigm. It is the foundation of the Christian religion that contains the words of God. The Bible gives direction and illustration how Christian must apply the Words of God to live right. The Bible contains great wisdom and truth that has been verified throughout history as being accurate. Their historical accounts are flawless, accurate and true.

I can say emphatically to my understanding of this great wisdom and truth of the Bible that Elijah mentored Elisha, Naomi mentored Ruth, and Mordecai mentored Esther and they all live a fulfill life that God designed. Your marriage mentor couple is your instructor, to reprove you when you fall out of line and constantly review your marriage situation so that you may have a marriage, a miracle of completion in Jesus name.

AMEN.

DECISION TIME

May I encourage you to accept Jesus Christ as your personal Lord and Savior today? "For if you confess with your mouth that Jesus is Lord and believe in your heart that God raised him from the dead, you will be saved." (Romans 10:9.)

Pray this prayer with me from your heart now!

"Lord Jesus, I believe that you died for me and rose again on the third day. I confess, I am a sinner and need your love and forgiveness. Come into my heart and forgive my sins. I receive your eternal life and confirm your love by giving me peace, joy and supernatural love for other people, in Jesus mighty name" Amen.

OTHER BOOKS BY;

Charles O. Soyoye

The Secrets of Living in the Will of God

The Scriptural Principles of Tithing and Offering blessing

The Spiritual Covenant of Prosperity Blessing

Available from your local bookstore!

I BELIEVE

Every married couple was designed for accomplishment,
Engineered for marital success,
And endowed with seeds of fruitfulness!

Lightning Source UK Ltd.
Milton Keynes UK
UKHW011836140919
349778UK00001B/23/P